Supporting Struggling Readers

BARBARA J. WALKER

Pippin Publishing

Copyright © 1992 by Pippin Publishing Corporation
85 Ellesmere Road
Suite 232
Scarborough, Ontario
M1R 4B9

Designed by John Zehethofer
Edited by Dyanne Rivers
Printed and bound in Canada by Friesens

Canadian Cataloguing in Publication Data

Walker, Barbara J., 1946-
    Supporting Struggling Readers

(The Pippin teacher's library ; 7)
Includes bibliographical references.
ISBN 0-88751-048-5

1. Reading — Remedial teaching.
I. Title. II. Series.

LB1050.5.W35 1992   372.4′3   C92-093887-6

ISBN 0-88751-048-5

10   9   8   7   6   5

CONTENTS

. . . .

INTRODUCTION

Readers of all descriptions work to make sense of the literacy events that crowd their lives. Struggling readers, too, work to make sense of literacy events, often in situations that inhibit, rather than support, their search for meaning. Nevertheless, they *are* active learners in search of meaning who deserve support as they struggle to make sense.

To help you understand and support their literacy development, this book will illustrate:

— An interactive view of the reading process.
— How individual processing, coupled with inappropriate instruction, often reinforces inappropriate literacy strategies.
— A developmental view of literacy.
— Instructional methods and authentic assessment procedures to enable us to work together to support struggling readers as they develop.

As you read, I hope you will come to appreciate that struggling readers do attempt to make sense of what they read, and that they do so by using what they can already do. Too often, instruction focuses on what they can't do, leaving them struggling to make sense of what they're reading and writing. But if teachers support the literacy development of struggling readers by joining them in focusing on what they can do, they are able to construct meaning successfully from text.

In the following pages, you'll find suggestions that will enable you to offer this support.

ACTIVE LITERACY

Being literate means that children and adults are able to use reading and writing to make sense of their world. As we communicate with one another, we use a multitude of strategies to make sense. Depending on the situation, readers have different purposes for reading and these affect both the strategies we use and our interpretation of the text. For example, a young man was reading a manual as he repaired a motor in auto mechanics class. He read a few paragraphs, looked at a diagram, then worked on the engine. Later that day, he sat reading a magazine for an extended period. The reading strategies he used on these two occasions changed because his purpose had changed — from reading to perform a task to reading for enjoyment.

Readers also vary their strategies as the text organization changes. In the case of the young man, for example, the text changed from a manual with diagrams to a magazine for leisure reading.

Because readers' knowledge of various topics differs, their level of understanding changes with the topic. A myriad of factors — the strategies possessed, purpose for reading, knowledge of the topic, format of the text and situational context — affects their ability to make sense of language. The level of success or difficulty experienced by a reader, then, results from an interaction among these factors. Difficulty is not the result of a fixed deficit within a reader. For example, a group of children from Calgary read and understood a difficult passage about glaciers because they had just returned from the Columbia Icefields where they had seen how glaciers formed. On the other hand, this same group of children had a great deal of difficulty when they read an easier passage about tropical rain forests. In these two instances, the students had not changed — the text had. Their difficulty interpreting the passage about rain forests resulted not from an underlying cognitive deficit, but simply from a lack of familiarity with the topic.

Both the readers' ability and the difficulty of a literacy activity are considered relative. No longer considered a static characteristic, reading difficulty is contingent on the interaction among a unique reader, a text and instruction. A closer look at the active process of constructing meaning helps us understand both reading proficiency and difficulty. This process involves readers in predicting, checking and elaborating on their interpretation within a particular situation. This chapter will take a closer look at the active process of making sense of text.

Predicting

Readers predict what the text will say using what they already know. They use this strategy, as well as the textual information, to make sense of what they're reading. As they read, they develop patterns based on their previous knowledge to give themselves clues. Just as a weather forecaster uses an array of instruments to predict the weather, readers use an array of information sources to predict what the text is likely to say. These knowledge sources, such as the features and meaning of words, sentence organization and the organization of the text, are used in combination with readers' previous grammatical knowledge and familiarity with the topic to facilitate understanding.

When reading a passage about a roller coaster ride, for example, they might say to themselves, I know what this is going to say, because I've been on a roller coaster ride. In this way, they predict what the text is going to say. Like the weather forecaster's predictions, theirs are sometimes accurate, sometimes not.

Checking Predictions

Active literacy involves not only making predictions, but also checking those predictions. Readers continually check their understanding to see if it makes sense. As they read more text, they might say to themselves, Yes, that is exactly how I felt when I rode the roller coaster, or, Oops, this character didn't have the same experience as I did. This internal dialogue allows readers to monitor their understanding. They check both the text and their own previous knowledge to figure out what went wrong. Then, they revise their understanding and continue to read. Like the weather forecaster, they continually check data from a variety of sources, revising and refining their original predictions.

Developing readers check their understanding by asking themselves questions that direct their use of fix-up strategies. They reread to correct misunderstandings or check their own previous knowledge. As this active process of predicting and revising continues, children begin to reflect on the topic they're reading about, the structure of the text and the strategies they're using. This leads to further elaborations.

Expanding Strategies and Understanding of Content

As students read and write, they elaborate on what and how they read. They might say to themselves about a passage, Hey, I get this because it's like the octopus ride at the fair. They make associations between what they already know and the new information in the passage and these new associations become part of what they know. Thus, reading and writing become tools for consolidating information and identifying strategies.

As weather forecasters encounter new phenomena, they can more easily identify a particular pattern when they see it a second and third time. In the same way, by participating in extensive literacy activities, readers learn to identify patterns in text and their own knowledge. They write about their reading and reconstruct information, tying it to what they already know. Thus, writing helps readers expand their knowledge of a topic and think about how the information fits what they already know. This helps them remember and interpret what and how they are reading.

Situating Literacy

Readers are constantly expanding their repertoire of strategies for dealing with text. As they do so, they think about the situation in which the literacy event occurred, another characteristic of active literacy. The social aspects of literacy influence developing readers' attitudes, their definition of literacy, and the strategies they use. For example, the young child listening to a parent read a story is involved in a social experience that transfers meaning to printed language. The parent conveys meaning by reading with expression and emotion. As the parent and child talk about the words on the page, they create a social interaction that affects the child's perceptions of literacy.

These same interactions continue into the culture of the school. In fact, school has become a culture of its own. Like parents, teachers are an integral part of the literacy context, orchestrating it and negotiating meaning among class members. For example, one struggling third-grade girl asked her teacher, "When do I get out of the group with all the boys?" Her membership in this group of readers experiencing difficulty was limiting her reading development as well as that of the boys. Group membership often defines who gets to do what and can limit literacy development.

The circumstances in which reading occurs direct developing readers' purposes and frame their perspectives about literacy events. For example, a young student in a foods class became involved in writing a report on lime. However, she forgot to check the context and wrote an extensive report on lime, the stone. The next day, she walked into the foods class, assessed the context and realized that the report should have been on lime, the fruit.

Readers constantly use their knowledge of the situation to select both their strategies and the information they use. Thus, circumstances affect what developing readers perceive as important, how sources are combined, what is elaborated on and how strategies are selected, as well as their perceptions about the literacy event.

The Model

This model shows the previously discussed aspects of the reading process as they interact continuously while developing readers construct meaning.

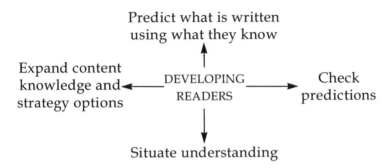

Developing readers predict what the text will say by linking sources of information (previous knowledge and the text) and checking — as well as revising when necessary — their predictions and interpretations. As they read, they add to their knowledge about the topic and elaborate on the strategies they used. Within each literacy event, knowledge is reconstructed as the learner reflects on how a particular context affected his interpretation. As students read and write, resolving ambiguities in a variety of literacy contexts, they refine and generalize their knowledge and strategies. As a result, these are constantly evolving.

Summary

To summarize, then, we reviewed the following four aspects of the interactive view of reading:

- Developing readers use many sources of information to predict what the text will say.
- Developing readers automatically monitor their interpretation of the text by checking their predictions against the text.
- Developing readers expand their content knowledge and strategy options by embedding new information and strategies within existing knowledge.

— Developing readers select strategies and expand their knowledge of a topic depending on the situation — academic, recreational, etc. — they encounter.

. . . .

REASONS

FOR READING DIFFICULTY

All readers use what they can already do to work out difficulties they encounter as they read and write. When a task calls for them to use strategies that are unfamiliar or that they can't perform, they avoid these. Instead, they fall back on what they can already do. For this reason, readers who are continually placed in situations where learning is difficult develop inappropriate compensatory strategies. Rather than double-checking the text, some will guess wildly at words, using what they think the text might say and actually creating a new story. Others, who are unfamiliar with a topic, will read strings of words, hoping for something to make sense. They don't check their own knowledge to look for ways to connect what they're reading to what they already know. Using these inappropriate alternative strategies often causes parents and teachers to view these students as less able to engage in literacy activities.

Believing these students to be less capable, teachers often reduce the quantity and quality of instruction, increasing the likelihood that struggling readers will be placed in learning situations where they'll develop inappropriate compensatory strategies. And so the cycle continues.

When students repeatedly find themselves in situations where their natural sense-making strategies are at odds with the instruction they receive, they begin to rely solely on these inappropriate alternative strategies to construct meaning. This reliance hinders their literacy development and their reading becomes unproductive. For example, beginning readers who rely on their personal knowledge rather than textual clues may be fairly successful — at first. Eventually, however, they'll find themselves in situations where they must predict using personal knowledge, then check the words in the text. If they're inattentive and randomly select letters when doing this checking, they'll find the strategy doesn't work. As a result, it will be abandoned as they begin to rely solely on their personal knowledge and pictures. In other words, they will shift away from a particular information source rather than integrating it and linking sources. Because this strategy is built on what they can already do, they will be fairly successful for a time, continuing to use the limited strategy rather than developing more flexible strategies.

As indicated by this example, the interactive model of reading can set up a framework for studying reading difficulty. Reading difficulty develops when students frequently rely on a single source of information rather than linking sources, repeatedly read hard passages that restrict the growth of knowledge and strategies, read without checking meaning, a practice that results in the development of limited rather than flexible strategies, and expect literacy activities to result in failure. Thus, reading difficulty is not a characteristic that lies solely within the student; rather, it is influenced by a variety of factors that interact during each literacy event.

Difficulty Linking Sources of Information

At the onset of literacy, children learn to link sources of information. Often, however, struggling readers exhibit a deficiency in either a skill, such as sight word knowledge, or an ability, such as sound blending, that causes them to shift away from an information source.

In an essay that appeared in *The Handbook of Reading Research*, Richard Allington says, "Poor beginning readers...seem to rely on one available source of information rather than integrating all available cues." These readers experience difficulty because they don't link sources of information. For example, readers who have difficulty with sound blending may rely on what they know about the pictures rather than sounding out the letters. When the topic is familiar, this strategy may be productive. However, as they confront more unfamiliar topics and avoid looking at the text to sound out a few letters in the word, their interpretation becomes increasingly muddled. By relying solely on what they can already do — using background knowledge, in this instance — they develop inappropriate strategies. In essence, a strength becomes a weakness.

Here's another example. Sandy had trouble learning the sounds of letters in first grade. Although he had a wealth of experiences before he started school, learning to read became difficult because he used only his personal knowledge to help decode the text. He made many miscues that were impossible to correct because he couldn't sound out the words. Sandy continued to use his strength, personal knowledge, to figure out words. When this didn't work, he made up the story by looking at the pictures. If this strategy is used occasionally, Sandy will continue to progress, but if he constantly uses his own knowledge without linking it to the words of the story, his reading will become hesitant and halting because nothing will fit together.

On the other hand, Trish learned phonics easily and, like some struggling readers, believed reading consisted of calling words precisely. She assumed that the meaning is found entirely in the print. As stories became more complicated, she could no longer simply repeat the words in the text to indicate her understanding. Occasionally, this strategy will work. However, if Trish continues to read stories without making sense, her reading will falter.

TEACHING STRATEGIES

For these readers, teachers use regular classroom materials or modifications to select instructional procedures that allow students to make sense of stories using what they already know and do. Later, they show these students how to link sources of information. In Sandy's case, for example, the following sequence builds on what he can already do to show him more appropriate strategies:

- To help develop his phonic awareness, Sandy reads several stories, primarily from predictable books with rhyming words.

- He writes a copy-cat story using the rhyming words in the stories to help him recognize word patterns.
- The teacher demonstrates a few rules of phonics by showing him how his knowledge of the rhyming words — a strength he has acquired — can help him decode unknown words by comparing them to known words. He might, for example, substitute initial consonants in rhyming words.

Sometimes, children like Sandy and Trish don't receive instruction that shows them how to link knowledge sources. In some special programs, the thrust is to identify weaknesses and concentrate on difficulties rather than identifying and consciously supporting strengths. In an environment divorced from authentic literacy activities, instruction is aimed at isolating weaknesses and providing drills that focus on specific skills. In these programs, children reach the required standard on the isolated skill assessments so they continue to read selections that are too hard for them, a situation that magnifies their difficulties. They cease to expand knowledge or strategies because few of their literacy endeavors make sense.

Difficulty Expanding Content and Strategy Knowledge

When children are continually expected to read demanding texts, they expend their energy constructing a hazy model of meaning. They do not expand their knowledge of the topic because they are too occupied trying to make sense of the story. Likewise, they do not organize their strategies so that they can readily apply them in other literacy activities. As Connie Juel found in a study reported in the *Journal of Educational Psychology*, struggling readers are, in fact, often expected to read extremely difficult material and to complete workbook pages to reinforce reading skills at the expense of reading whole stories. While children in high reading groups read extensively, encountering few unfamiliar words, struggling readers are asked to read about 50 per cent less and miss about every third word. When this happens, the gap between what struggling readers know and what they are asked to read is so great that they cannot organize either what or how they are reading. Instead, they rely on what they can already do, making sense of text only infrequently.

For example, Sandy does think about the topic, adding some new information to his background knowledge. But he avoids looking at the words on the page because they are difficult. He doesn't develop flexible procedures for figuring out unfamiliar words. Rather than linking information sources and figuring out how these sources can be used together, he relies only on his own background knowledge to figure out unfamiliar words. In the process, his reading becomes slower and less accurate until, finally, he begins reading word by word.

TEACHING STRATEGIES

What struggling readers like Sandy and Trish need is to read lots of authentic stories that are familiar enough for them to examine their trouble-shooting strategies. As students progress through literacy development, making the links between the words in the text and what they know about words becomes routine. This permits them to use more of their thinking capacity to organize thoughtful responses and concentrate on explaining their strategies as well as comprehending the topic.

In essence, fluent reading allows students to clarify the links between the text and the strategies they use to make sense of the text. When struggling readers are continually subjected to literacy experiences where they cannot read fluently, they become oblivious to the strategies they use and, in fact, are unable to integrate the meaning of new words that would, in turn, help them figure out unfamiliar words. They fail to develop an extensive network among sources of information. For readers like Sandy and Trish, the links among cognitive operations that occur for proficient readers break down. They rely exclusively on their strengths and fail to develop other strategies. Because so little of what they read makes sense, they passively read words without expecting anything to make sense.

Difficulty Monitoring Meaning

When students rely on their strengths without expanding their understanding, they grow accustomed to reading without making sense. As Page Bristow suggests in an article in *The Reading Teacher*, the infrequent use of appropriate strategies produces a muddled system for checking comprehension.

Struggling readers appear to lack strategies that good readers use naturally. When queried, they glumly reply, "I don't know." In reality, they really don't know how to restore their understanding. They did read the words and they knew that what they read didn't make sense, but they didn't know how to change this situation. Because these readers have little experience constructing meaning, they passively read words without actively questioning their understanding. For example, when reading aloud, they seldom correct their mistakes, answering questions by repeating the words exactly as they appear in the text. When reading for understanding, they seldom revise their predictions, sticking with their initial predictions even when there is no evidence to support them in the text.

For these readers, simply making the text easier or modifying a technique will not change the passive approach they have developed. In an article in *Learning Disability Quarterly*, Scott Paris and Evelyn Oka say that struggling readers remain "unconvinced of the importance or necessity of using strategies" even when these are demonstrated. For example, Sandy and Trish knew they didn't understand, but they didn't know how to regain meaning because they had used their inappropriate alternative strategies for so long. They really don't know what strategies are or how to apply them.

TEACHING STRATEGIES

Sandy and Trish need to see an example of how to think when they encounter difficulty. For instance, Trish needs to learn to say to herself, This is not making sense. I can change how I'm reading. I need to reread the last paragraph and think about what I know. After seeing an example, they need some coaching as they begin to use these new strategies.

Likewise, teachers need to help struggling readers identify strategies and see the relationship between the strategies they use and their interpretation of the text. For instance, when Trish and Sandy interpret text successfully, they need to talk about the strategies they used to construct meaning and think about how effective these strategies were. Sharing interpretations with their peers helps them think about how they arrived at their answers by combining their own knowledge with the information in the text. During a discussion like this, they also help each other evaluate the strategies they used. Shared discussions help them learn that the strategies they use, rather than their ability, affects their understanding.

Unfortunately, remedial programs have been based on specific skill packets and workbooks where progress is monitored according to the number of right and wrong answers to questions. When reading is reduced to mastering a skill that readers lack, they increasingly define reading as a no-win situation. Their passive reading behavior magnifies and they finally give up the whole miserable attempt.

Difficulty Translating the Situational Context

When students find themselves in literacy situations where they continually fail, they abandon their sense-making strategies and come to believe that they are doomed to failure. Struggling readers believe they don't have the ability to learn. They think to themselves, I will not try, because if I try and fail again, I am admitting I am dumb. Then, to preserve their sense of self-worth, they stop trying, thus eliminating the possibility of being dumb.

This attitude is perpetuated by the use of norm-referenced evaluations that reward students with above-average ability. For example, Sandy and Trish try hard, but they don't measure up to the criterion set by students who learn easily and quickly. Soon they realize that their efforts will not guarantee success. So Sandy and Trish create excuses for not having their work completed, thereby avoiding a sense of failure and regaining their self-worth by simply not trying. In fact, Sandy and Trish may never stay with a task long enough to discover that they can be successful.

Because they appear not to care about their own learning, their teacher decides they are lazy and unmotivated. But, as James Raffini points out in *Student Apathy: The Protection of Self-Worth*, Sandy and Trish are actually highly motivated — to preserve their sense of self-worth in the face of failure. Because of their repeated failures, the two have developed a fuzzy notion about both success and failure. They attribute their failure to being stupid, a characteristic that cannot be changed, and they cease to expend effort. When they do succeed, they maintain that it was because of the easy materials or their teachers' effort rather than their own.

Because teachers have often focused on skills that students don't possess and asked them to complete drill exercises in a one-to-one situation isolated from any discussion about the meaning of stories, struggling readers develop a two-pronged definition of reading:

— Reading is getting the answers right.
— Reading is something "I can't do."

Measuring themselves by this definition, these struggling readers judge themselves to be poor readers, reducing their motivation.

TEACHING STRATEGIES

What Sandy and Trish need is to build a perception of themselves as members of the literacy community. To do this, their teachers need to change the quality of the interactions within their classrooms. One way they can do this is by reviewing their own prompting behaviors. For instance, during oral reading, teachers often interrupt to give struggling readers a word as soon as they make an error, a tactic that conveys the message that these children are incapable of making sense out of the mistake. If, on the other hand, teachers treat struggling readers the same way as successful students by assisting so they can continue to the end of the sentence, they convey confidence in the children's ability to correct their interpretation.

In addition, teachers can ask struggling readers more questions that require them to make inferences and judgments, just as they do their achieving counterparts. As they ask these questions, they can also prompt struggling readers or give them hints, providing the opportunity for them to construct meaningful responses. As Madaline Will noted in *Educating Students with Learning Problems: A Shared Responsibility*, teachers often direct complex questions only to the more successful students, either giving struggling readers the answer or excusing them from difficult assignments. Furthermore, they are sometimes placed in special classes where they can't interact with achieving peers.

Teachers need to help struggling readers identify their strategies and see the relationship between the strategies they use, their interpretation of the text and the effort they expend. For example, when Trish and Sandy are successful, they need to assess the strategies they used as well as their effort. They need to be helped to define literacy as an active process that involves using the strategies they already possess.

Summary

In this chapter, we've looked at four reasons students experience reading difficulties:

— Struggling readers often rely on a single information source, shifting away from using strategies that haven't been successful.
— They're often asked to read difficult texts, placing them in a situation where they cannot readily integrate new information with their strategies.
— They read and write passively because much of what they're asked to read doesn't make sense to them.
— Struggling readers who have failed repeatedly perceive the literacy event as a failure situation, thus decreasing their motivation.

These reasons were explained in terms of an interaction between student behaviors and classroom instruction, illustrating the powerful influence teachers and schooling have on struggling readers.

GUIDELINES

FOR INSTRUCTION

Because instruction can augment or curb literacy development, we, as teachers, must be mindful of our instructional choices as we respond to the needs of struggling readers. We must think about how our instruction affects the way students perceive the context, link information sources, develop strategies and check their comprehension. Given what we know about the reasons children experience reading difficulties, this chapter suggests guidelines for teaching struggling readers.

Focus on What Children Can Do

Because struggling readers unconsciously shift away from a weakness and rely on what they can already do, the sensitive teacher creates literacy activities that encourage them to use strategies with which they are successful. For example, teachers can use a variety of prompts to encourage readers to use their natural abilities. One teacher was working with a child who could sound out words, but using this strategy alone caused him to read slowly and impaired his comprehension. As he stumbled over an unfamiliar word in a passage he was reading aloud, the teacher began by asking, "What would make sense and sounds like what you're saying?" This prompt allowed him to use his facility in sounding out words at the same time as he thought about what made sense in the context of the passage.

Sensitive teachers encourage students to use their strengths to solve difficulties, but they also ask them to use this strength in combination with other strategies. In *Stress and Reading Difficulties*, Lance Gentile and Mirna McMillan suggest that, because literacy activities are more stressful for struggling readers, they need to be reminded constantly that they possess natural strategies. By using instructional techniques that encourage children to demonstrate what they can already do, the teacher reduces this stress and fosters their literacy endeavors.

Use Familiar Topics

Because struggling readers encounter many experiences that are overly challenging, sensitive teachers ensure that they are asked to read material within their reading level that is familiar enough for them to engage in sense-making strategies. These stories need to be read with no more than one error every 10 words, a 90 per cent accuracy rate. At this rate, they are able to make sense of the text and engage in fix-up strategies. If they make more than one error every 10 words, they can't understand enough to correct their mistakes.

When choosing material, the teacher considers the students' reading performance and the extent of their previous experiences related to the topic. Along with the students, she chooses stories that are familiar enough that they can readily predict, monitor and expand on the content of the passage. Additionally, she carefully selects authentic texts so the children can identify with the main character's conflict and successfully predict solutions based on their own experiences. Likewise, she encourages students to write about their own experiences using familiar language. In this way, they generate longer and more well-formed texts. The more students read and write about familiar topics, the greater their understanding.

Focus on Making Sense

Many struggling readers become so involved in decoding individual words that they forget to make sense out of what they are reading. However, from a very young age, children strive to make sense of their world and the sensitive teacher builds on this natural curiosity by supporting students in making sense of reading and writing activities. In their search for meaning, developing readers invent their own explanations, examine and justify these reasons, and finally rework their explanations.

Many times, it is the language of teaching that encourages a "making-sense" perspective. Even a teacher's non-verbal behavior can empower students to make sense of text. One first-grade teacher communicates this message by simply scratching her head in wonderment when something a student says doesn't make sense. Some teachers use questions like, "Did that make sense?" Others combine prompts, always from the perspective that the words must make sense: "What makes sense (overall meaning) and begins with the letter 'f' (printed text)?"

During a discussion of a story, the line of questioning can communicate the expectation that the words will make sense. If teachers ask a string of unrelated questions aimed at eliciting only facts, students develop the idea that the purpose of reading is to get the facts right rather than construct meaningful responses. Sensitive teachers prepare a discussion and questions that will lead struggling readers to construct a cohesive view of the story. In all their instruction, sensitive teachers build on the students' natural inclination to make sense of the world.

Ask Children What They Want to Learn

Engaging struggling readers in structured learning activities can be tricky. Because they have experienced failure, whether in the short- or long-term, they are extremely skeptical of any activity that a *teacher* might suggest. Because of this, Page Bristow explains in an article in *The Reading Teacher*, it is critical that they participate in defining the goals of their literacy activities. This doesn't mean that students are free to roam the halls rather than completing activities. It does mean that they have the opportunity to choose among selected options. Teachers can engage them in defining what they want to know in several ways.

— Students can select the topic or reading material. As they select their reading material or activity, they begin to define their own reasons for reading.
— Students can assess their own literacy and decide on goals for their own learning. In this way, they evaluate their own progress towards strategic literacy.
— Students can read and write for their own purposes during uninterrupted time periods.

When students are asked to identify what they want to learn, the teacher is helping them make a personal investment in the outcome of literacy activities.

Ask Children What They Already Know

Struggling readers often know a great deal about a subject, but forget to use this knowledge when they read, acting as if answers magically emerge from school books. Because school-related task seem unrelated to life in general, they leave their knowledge at home. But reading and writing about what you know is critical to engaging actively in literacy activities.

Sensitive teachers ask students what they know about topics and help them actively use this information as they read. For example, a young middle-school student read a story about a young girl whose father always let her have her way. In interpreting the story, he could not predict what would happen even though his experience in his own family, where his sister always got her way, was similar. When the teacher asked him about the interactions in his home and if there were any similarities between them and the story, he was slowly able to begin to use his own experience to interpret the actions of the main character.

Struggling readers often need help figuring out when and how to use what they already know. As they lead discussions about stories, sensitive teachers think about each child's experiences and how these can be used.

Discuss Whole Stories in Group Settings

Often struggling readers receive extensive skills instruction in isolated situations where the sole interaction is with the teacher about the correctness of their responses. Instructional situations like this inhibit the development of a sense of story and how language works. Developing readers benefit from situations in which they read and write about complete stories because doing so helps them internalize how written language and stories work. When they understand the structure of printed language, they have less difficulty interpreting stories by shifting between what they already know and the text.

Not only do students need to read whole stories, but they also need to discuss them. During discussions, students share their interpretations, focus their purposes and think about the functions of reading and writing. They discuss how they constructed their responses, justifying their interpretations based on the story as well as what they know. Thus, readers need experiences where they can discuss their thinking about a topic in both small- and large-group settings.

Revisit Text

Struggling readers have difficulty expanding their knowledge of content and of the strategies they use. Revisiting texts helps them do both. When they reread a passage, the structure of the text and the topic are already familiar so they can make connections between what they already know and the information presented in the text. This allows for a deeper processing of the information. Not only can they expand their knowledge of the topic, but they can also think about how they are constructing their interpretation. Research indicates that rereading increases fluent, strategic reading and this helps students use more effective trouble-shooting strategies by giving them time to think. The sensitive teacher creates authentic activities for revisiting text, allowing struggling readers to expand their knowledge of both the topic and their strategies.

Coach Literate Behaviors

Because struggling readers have continually experienced reading without making sense, they are unaware of when and how to use strategies as they read and write. Sensitive teachers act as coaches by observing the strategic behaviors of students, then explaining and demonstrating thinking that will augment the strategies they're using. In these instances, the teacher thinks aloud about how he would remedy a particular difficulty. For example, one child continued to answer questions using only information from the text. The teacher began by recalling the textual information himself, then demonstrated how he thought about this information using his own previous knowledge. He asked the child to relate similar experiences, then construct a response.

This coaching in how to think involves demonstrating procedures for removing difficulties in making interpretations. To do this, the teacher purposely makes mistakes while reading so he can demonstrate how he monitors his own active search for meaning. Too often, struggling readers perceive literacy as error-free reading and correct writing. By making mistakes, the teacher shows students his own coping behaviors and that mistakes are valuable tools for learning rather than indications of failure.

This demonstration and the subsequent coaching helps struggling readers develop a risk-taking attitude toward literacy events. As students talk about how they solve problems, the teacher has an opportunity to provide support and feedback about their thinking. He provides encouragement by commenting on their trouble-shooting behavior, possibly saying something like, "I noticed the way you used your knowledge about Africa to figure out that the country was Egypt." When coaching this way, the teacher phases in to support effective strategies and phases out to allow children to think independently, gradually increasing the time he waits before offering support so that the children have time to develop responses. When offering support, the teacher probes the children's reasoning by using parts of their answers to demonstrate thinking.

Ask Children What They Learned

Because they continually experience failure, struggling readers develop a hazy evaluation of both their successes and failures. Sensitive teachers help these students develop a realistic assessment of their literate behavior by asking them to describe how they think and read. This self-assessment helps readers recognize their successes as well as the strategies they use. The teacher discusses the relationship between their effort, use of strategies and successful interpretations of the text. These discussions can be supported in several ways:

— Inviting children to choose what is included in their assessment portfolio can help them evaluate their success in various activities and show them their progress over time.

— Students can also evaluate their success in individual literacy activities. By using a checksheet for story summaries, students can evaluate their own summaries, deciding whether they set out the main characters, setting, problem, major events and problem resolution. Using the checksheet, the students and teacher assess literacy together.

— Students can discuss the strategies they use and the effort expended. One teacher discusses effective reading strategies and effort by charting key aspects of the prediction process. After reading a story, students rate their predictions using the following chart. The chart is supplemented by a summary sentence that includes an assessment of the relationship between effort and strategy use.

Today's Evaluation

1 = Not Good   2 = Okay   3 = Good   4 = Very Good

I made predictions.	1 2 3 4
Most of my predictions used only what I knew.	1 2 3 4
Most of my predictions used only what the text said.	1 2 3 4
Most of my predictions used both what the text said and what I knew.	1 2 3 4

Assessments like this help struggling readers attribute their performance to intrinsic factors such as their own knowledge and skill at using strategies rather than to luck or easy materials. In their article in *Journal of Reading Behavior*, Peter Johnston and Peter Winogard write, "Self-assessment can force attention to the details of outcomes, and to the effects of the use of various strategies." As students identify and assess the problem-solving strategies they use, they can attribute their success to these strategies rather than to abilities they believe they don't possess.

Support Children's Membership in the Literacy Community

Struggling readers often find themselves at odds with literacy activities, viewing literacy as something they don't possess. As Frank Smith says in his book, *Joining the Literacy Club,* sensitive teachers ensure that all children view themselves as members of the literacy community by inviting children to participate in collaborative and meaningful literacy. Time is set aside each day for personal reading and writing when students can read books they have selected themselves for their own purposes and write about their own ideas. Likewise, time is set aside to share ideas and interpretations gained from personal reading and writing.

When doing this, teachers and students share their own interpretations and queries, creating an environment in which everyone takes risks while constructing meaning. It is important for teachers to share their own personal responses as readers and writers so they, too, are viewed as members of the literacy community.

Summary

Using these guidelines, teachers can build an effective instructional program that supports struggling readers as they make sense of text. By building on what children can already do using familiar topics, they ensure that the children experience success. Asking children what they want to learn as well as what they already know involves them in the literacy activities. Likewise, discussing whole stories with their peers allows them to share interpretations and strategies in a situation where the activities make sense. As children revisit text and benefit from the teacher's coaching, they extend their trouble-shooting behaviors and begin to take more risks. And, as teachers ask children what they learned and include them in the literacy community, they begin to view themselves as readers and writers. These guidelines are valuable tools that experienced teachers use to support the literacy of all readers.

. . . .

LITERACY DEVELOPMENT —

A CONTINUING PROCESS

Just as individuals pass through a series of phases as they develop physically, they also progress through phases of literacy development, learning to talk, then read and write. Specific characteristics are associated with each developmental phase and these present challenges that must be met if growth is to continue.

The five stages of literacy development — emergent, grounded, expanding, strategic and reflective — are not separate from each other, nor are their boundaries sharply defined. Rather, they overlap, as each grows out of the previous phase. The diagram on the following page illustrates this overlap.

As developing readers encounter more difficult passages, they use the active learning process to decode the text and develop new generalizations about literacy. Rather than concentrating solely on the new task, they refine and build on their experience with previous tasks, fitting the resulting insights into the new framework as it develops.

During the transition from one phase to the next, critical learning occurs and this enhances future literacy development. The challenges encountered during this time lead to new thinking and increased interactions among literacy behaviors.

This chapter provides an overview of the five stages of literacy development and suggests teaching strategies that can be used during each phase. Both the stages and teaching strategies will be discussed in greater detail in subsequent chapters. Because literacy development flows along a continuum, it's worth remembering that none of the teaching strategies need be restricted to a particular phase. Rather, instruction needs to focus on individual readers and their development.

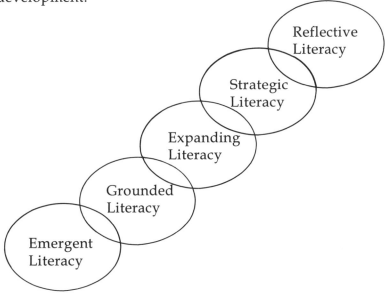

Emergent Literacy

During the emergent literacy phase, children become aware of the symbols in their environment, learning, for example, that the golden arches represent McDonalds. This kind of recognition — that a symbol represents a familiar concept — sets the stage for the early beginning of print awareness. As parents read and reread stories to them, children begin to associate the symbols on the printed page with the words their parents are saying and, indeed, often memorize their favorite books. When they write their names, they learn that the pattern of letters in words is consistent. As they integrate these experiences, young readers use their knowledge of the social context, such as memorizing stories with Mom and Dad, to figure out how print works. This phase is often referred to as emerging literacy because the literacy behaviors seem to emerge naturally out of the experiences of young children — without formal instruction.

At school, teachers try to emulate these early experiences by using the language experience approach and shared reading to create situations that help developing readers make associations between what is said and what is written. As the teacher creates an experience, she situates the literacy event and then writes down the language. Developing readers use their understanding of the situation to figure out the words in the story.

Grounded Literacy

As developing readers begin to encounter unfamiliar words and longer stories, they develop new strategies to meet this challenge. As their literacy development becomes grounded in textual conventions, their comprehension will rely less on understanding the social context. For example, when they double-check the text to verify their understanding, they must examine the print, looking closely at the patterns of letters and words. To figure out unfamiliar words in new stories, they might think to themselves, What makes sense and looks like this word? As their literacy activities shift from predominantly oral, shared reading to silent reading and discussion, youngsters are asked to reflect their overall understanding of the story by discussing what they read. These activities require developing readers to ground their literacy in textual conventions so that more fluent reading and thinking can develop.

TEACHING STRATEGIES

To help focus developing readers' attention on the structure of the text and ground their literacy in the conventions of the text, teachers can encourage them to write copy-cat stories and make story frames. To complete these activities, they must think about the letters in words and about how the story is formed.

Expanding Literacy

As developing readers ground their literacy in textual conventions, they lose fluency. Therefore, the challenge of the expanding literacy phase is to broaden children's literacy so they are equipped to associate their knowledge of both print and a particular topic with what is written on the page. As they progressed through the first two phases, they developed extensive knowledge of the conventions of print, both in words and in stories. Now their focus shifts from developing this knowledge to using it as they read. They need to link sources rapidly so their fluency in word identification integrates with their fluency in developing ideas. During the expanding literacy phase, fluent reading using sentence sense is the central focus of instruction. In particular, students learn that groups of words make meaning and sentences have predictable structures that influence meaning.

TEACHING STRATEGIES

During the expanding literacy phase, teachers often invite children to participate in story circles and readers' theater to focus their attention on connecting meaning and words simultaneously. To create a response, developing readers must think about how words and sentence structure influence meaning. Because they are encouraged to extend their literacy behaviors, these activities expand the literacy of developing readers.

Strategic Literacy

As students become adept at applying familiar strategies, they face a new challenge. During the strategic literacy phase, they assert new control over their thinking as they begin experimenting with ways of thinking about the process they use to construct meaning. This new phase of "thinking about thinking" allows them to take control of their comprehension and plan the probable outcomes of procedures related to how they construct an answer. As they take control of their strategies for learning, they interpret things from a personal point of view, which allows them to experiment with their ideas and thoughts about the world.

During the strategic literacy phase, teachers can use self-directed questioning and readers' workshops to focus children's attention on personal reading strategies and interpretations. Both these techniques ask students to construct personal meaning and analyze how they constructed it, differentiating their own knowledge from the author's meaning. To create their responses, they learn to control their ideas and separate them from those of the author. These activities help developing readers take control of their personal literacy strategies and interpretations. This personal fascination continues until these readers begin to meet new challenges.

Reflective Literacy

The final challenge of developing readers is to use reading and writing as tools to construct and communicate meaning. In the reflective literacy phase, they begin to look beyond their own point of view and recognize that others exist. During this phase of literacy, children select critical information from various sources to extend their own point of view. Using this information, they justify their point of view and distinguish it from that of others. To support their position, they synthesize information from various literary sources. They also summarize critical information and organize it in order to remember it. Finally, they communicate their thinking through both speaking and writing.

During the reflective literacy phase, teachers can use the opinion-proof technique and graphic organizers to focus readers' attention on thinking about what is important to remember and justifying their point of view. Both these techniques ask children to use their personal understanding to organize textual information. Developing readers learn to justify their selection of important concepts and explain how they synthesized the information.

Summary

Literacy development occurs in overlapping phases that flow along a continuum. Moving through the five phases — emergent literacy, grounded literacy, expanding literacy, strategic literacy and reflective literacy — can take a lifetime. Understanding the challenges of each phase increases the likelihood that teachers can help struggling readers meet the present challenge and subsequently lead them into even more challenging activities.

The chapters that follow provide more detailed information about each phase, pinpoint difficulties readers might encounter and suggest instructional strategies to help overcome these. These strategies need not be limited to a particular phase but may be used during all phases of development for very different reasons. Sensitive teachers analyze each teaching technique to evaluate how it can be used to advance a reader's development.

. . . .

EMERGENT LITERACY

During the emergent literacy phase, readers combine what they already know with the situational context to predict — and check — the meaning of printed symbols. As they do so, they acquire knowledge about written language. They use this information to figure out what the words on the page say.

Difficulties

When developing readers use only what they can already do to help them decode text, they run into trouble. Some rely too much on their own knowledge, without matching what they say to what the text on the page says. They seem to know so much that they are unconcerned with printed words. Others run into difficulty because they rely only on the situation to help them. This may, for example, involve listening to the rhythm and intonation of stories read aloud without matching what they hear to the words on the page. When they make miscues, they look to the teacher, rather than the text, to supply the correct word. In doing so, they are relying exclusively on the context rather than developing multiple strategies for identifying words.

Other struggling readers simply don't have enough background knowledge to make sense of the text. They repeat what the teacher says without understanding what they are reading. They often end up reading word by word, hoping against hope that something will make sense.

Instructional Strategies

The following instructional strategies emphasize building on the children's strengths to help them move towards literate behaviors. The strategies that will be discussed are the language experience approach, using predictable books in a shared reading setting, using talking books, choral reading and the thematic approach, as well as developing a reading recovery program. While these are suggestions for meeting the needs of struggling readers during this phase, they may be used during other phases for very different reasons. Sensitive teachers evaluate how a particular technique improves literacy for each individual child.

LANGUAGE EXPERIENCE

Some developing readers rely exclusively on their previous topic knowledge to help them decode text. To build on their natural ability to use oral language to communicate and on their background knowledge, teachers invite these students to dictate stories about everyday experiences. The teacher records the story on a large piece of paper and, when it is finished, reads it with the child to check content.

Then, teacher and child read the story several times together, providing the youngster with an opportunity to connect her background knowledge with the printed words. Each child then reads the story on her own and draws a picture to accompany it. In this way, the story becomes the instructional text and a collection of stories can become a reader.

There is a danger that some children will rapidly memorize the story they dictate and continue to focus on the social aspects of the literacy event rather than looking closely at the text. When this happens, teachers can copy chunks of the story onto cards and ask the children to read these in the order they appeared in the story. If they have trouble recognizing a word or phrase, the teacher prompts by asking questions like, "What did you say in the story after...?" or "You said, '(repeats the preceding section),' and then what did you say in the story?" These cues focus on the shift between oral and printed language. By building on their natural strengths, this approach helps struggling readers decode the printed words.

Some developing readers become so involved in the social context that they fail to look at the text. They might, for example, dictate elaborate stories to the teacher, then be unable to read what they said. For these — and other developing readers — using predictable books in a shared reading setting facilitates their fluency as well as their ability to identify words.

The teacher and children choose a predictable book, often a big book, that has a rhythmic, repetitive language pattern. Together, they read the book, with the teacher taking the lead during the first reading.

The teacher and children read the book several more times. During the second and third readings, the teacher begins to leave out words that can be predicted from the language pattern. For example, "I can hug my sister. I can hug my ...." Using their sense of language patterns, the children supply the missing word (in this case, "brother"). Eventually, they take over the reading of the story from the teacher.

Afterwards, the children read the book on their own. The teacher can phase in at any time to assist if they stumble over the language pattern.

When reading predictable books, children use their knowledge of the topic, story structure and language patterns to predict what the text will say. When they make a miscue, the teacher offers prompts like, "Remember the pattern...and look at the picture. Now what would this phrase say?" Or he may simply prompt with, "This phrase is about a dog. How would the pattern go?" This helps struggling readers use their sense of the patterns of language to figure out unfamiliar words.

CHORAL READING

Some developing readers like choral reading, where stories or poems are read aloud in unison, because it gives them an opportunity to follow the lead of the teacher or the group within a social context. They benefit from hearing the intonation and rhythm of a passage as more experienced readers demonstrate fluent, expressive oral reading.

The teacher and children select an engaging, but challenging, short story or poem and read it in unison, with the more capable readers reading ahead and slightly more loudly. All the children follow the words on the printed page. Afterwards, individual children can read the passage to the teacher who can supply difficult words, if necessary.

This technique places reading in a social context and allows the struggling reader to hear as well as read the message. It works particularly well for children who have been frustrated by their previous reading experiences. Although it is similar to techniques used with the language experience and shared reading approaches, choral reading is more flexible because it can be used with any kind of text. When they experience difficulty, readers can discuss the meaning with the teacher and read the selection chorally again. This places the selection in the social, rather than the printed, context.

THEMATIC APPROACH

Some developing readers have only limited experiences of the world and of using language to draw on. In many cases, the experience they do possess is difficult to connect to the stories that are used in school. Because they don't readily use language, their language experience stories are not well-developed.

Teachers can create literacy activities around extended themes to bolster the language and experiential resources of these children. This approach helps them construct a network of knowledge related to a particular topic. Children can draw on this knowledge when reading.

Once the theme is selected, the teacher needs to collect a variety of related reading material. She reads this aloud to the children, querying them about and discussing what they've learned.

After reading several books on the topic, the teacher and students work together to generate lists of what they've learned. These can be used to create a book or report about the theme and this becomes their reading text.

The children and teacher continue in this fashion, creating books about topics that are similar to the original theme. For instance, a group of young aboriginal students lacked the knowledge of English necessary to read stories in predictable books or create their own stories. Their teacher read aloud several books about a buffalo hunt, showed pictures of a hunt and encouraged the children to talk about hunting buffalo. The children then created a book about buffalo hunting. Then they read and wrote stories about hunting deer. Finally, they read and wrote about a lion hunt in Africa. In their theme books, the children used the same basic vocabulary, developing a background of experiences with both the content and print. If they were unable to identify a word, the teacher asked them to think about the other stories they had read to help figure it out. This encouraged them to build a network of meaning that they could draw on to help them identify words and expand their knowledge of the topic.

TALKING BOOKS

Some developing readers need to hear a story repeatedly so they can remember both the words and the sequence of events. Talking books, which are prerecorded readings of selected stories, help young readers associate what they hear with the text by providing them with the opportunity to hear and read a story many times.

The teacher and child select a book and tape that are interesting and short enough to complete in a single session. The child listens to and reads along with the tape until he can read the story fluently on his own. Once he can do so, he reads it orally to the teacher, who evaluates his oral reading, fluency and comprehension.

As they listen to and read talking books, children memorize the story and use this experience to anticipate what the words will be. Their familiarity with the story allows them to attend to both the meaning and the print at the same time. If they have difficulty, the teacher can read aloud the passage so they can hear the intonation and relate it to the message. The teacher also encourages them to listen to the story again, paying particular attention to the difficult sections.

This technique allows struggling readers to use the overall meaning of the story to figure out unknown words and frees the teacher to work with other children while those experiencing difficulty are listening to the tape.

READING RECOVERY

Reading recovery is actually an intervention program rather than an instructional technique. However, it has proven extremely effective with first-grade struggling readers who receive an individual 30-minute lesson every day in addition to regular classroom instruction.

In *The Early Detection of Reading Difficulties*, Marie Clay suggests that each session start with a reading of a familiar story. This encourages fluent, rhythmic reading that helps the child both experience what it feels like to read expressively and develop her reading strategies.

A new book, selected because the language structures in the text match the child's, is then introduced using the shared reading approach. The teacher and child review and discuss the story, paying particular attention to the story line. The teacher explains unfamiliar concepts using the language structure of the text, thus increasing the likelihood that the child will be able to read successfully on her own. As she reads the story again, the teacher assists as necessary, using as many meaning-focused prompts as possible.

Afterwards, the child writes a one- or two-sentence message, a technique described in greater detail in the next chapter. These are often accumulated over time and become a story.

Throughout the sessions, the teacher monitors the child's reading strategies daily by asking her to read a book that has been read only once before as the teacher records miscues. This information is used to guide the prompting behavior the teacher uses during the instructional session as well as to measure the child's progress towards proficient reading.

Summary

The teaching strategies suggested in this chapter are examples of practices that have been used with struggling readers during the emergent phase of literacy. Most of them rely strongly on showing these readers how to move beyond relying on the social context of literacy so they can begin decoding the words themselves.

. . . .

GROUNDED LITERACY

While children in the emergent phase of literacy use what they already know to help them decode text, they begin to ground their literacy in the text itself when they enter the next phase. In the grounded literacy phase, they use their sense of oral language to discover the patterns in written language. As they encounter more and more unfamiliar text while reading, they need strategies to help them figure out these words. At the same time, they must also develop their knowledge of how stories work. During this phase, literacy activities shift from predominantly oral, shared reading to silent reading and discussion. This shift means that students must be able to discuss what they read, drawing on their understanding of the plot and sequence of events in a story. It also requires developing readers to ground their literacy in textual conventions so that more fluent reading and thinking can develop.

Difficulties

During this phase, developing readers may experience difficulty because they have weaknesses that inhibit the natural evolution of their decoding strategies. Some readers, who have difficulty unlocking the patterns of sounds in words, continue using only their background knowledge, which fails them as they encounter unfamiliar passages more and more often. Others have difficulty following the story line, which means they have trouble when asked to predict what might happen next or discuss what they read.

Instructional Strategies

Instructional activities for children in the grounded literacy phase are directed towards processing both print and meaning. This processing focuses on the structure of text as readers ground their literacy in textual conventions.

To develop a sense of the code, developing readers must write, write, write. Although direct instruction in decoding will help them understand the code, writing allows for the natural evolution of the knowledge of written conventions. As students write, they develop an understanding that groups of letters form words and that these groups follow patterns.

Message writing, copy-cat stories and repeated readings are techniques that highlight this decoding within a meaningful context. Both writing and repeated reading help children shift their attention to the words in the text and focus attention on the structure of the stories.

As developing readers shift from oral to silent reading, they need to understand the framework of a story. This knowledge helps them predict what the author will say next and retell the story. Instructional strategies encouraging children to retell stories and create story frames and character maps help them develop a sense of text structure when reading. The following techniques have been used effectively with struggling readers during this phase of literacy development.

MESSAGE WRITING

Some struggling readers, who begin to read by making up the text to fit pictures, become so involved in predicting meaning this way that they fail to check the words on the page. Message writing can help them focus on the letters in words.

The teacher provides a blank writing book in which the pages are divided in half, the top half for practice and the bottom for the message. The child thinks up a one- or two-sentence message and writes it by slowing saying the words in order to predict the letters they include. If he doesn't know the printed form of a word, he goes to the practice section of the page and the teacher assists by drawing a box for each letter. The child slowly voices the sounds and places the letters he knows in the appropriate boxes. Then the teacher prints the unknown letters where they belong and the child copies the new word into the message. When finished, he reads the entire message.

As children predict letters in words, they attend to the pattern of the letters, a strategy that transfers to reading stories. When they make a miscue, the teacher asks them to notice the letters and the word length as well as the overall textual meaning. The teacher also draws comparisons with words they have written in the messages. In this way, children develop their sense of the pattern of letters in words.

COPY-CAT STORIES

Some struggling readers, who are unfamiliar with the patterns in words, also need a structure to help them write. Because they guess at words without checking their guesses against the text or their background knowledge, their predictions often don't make sense. These struggling readers profit from focusing on the text in both their reading and writing. Using familiar predictable books, students can create a new story using the pattern in the book. This allows them to take minimal risks and focuses their attention on the patterns within the words as well as in language.

Using the shared reading approach, the teacher reads aloud a predictable book. Afterwards, the teacher demonstrates how to create a new story following the pattern in the book and changing either the main character or the setting. The children and teacher create a new story together, then each child writes her own version of the predictable book.

By using most of the words from the predictable book, children are able to begin writing in a risk-free situation where they focus on the patterns of words and language. If even this task seems too demanding, the teacher can construct a predictable frame for the child by deleting the main character, but keeping the rest of the story the same. For instance, she could write, "There was an old _____ who swallowed a fly." As the child gets better at filling in the blanks, the teacher leaves out more and more of the story. For example, she might write, "There was an old _____ who _____ a _____."

Copy-cat stories help struggling readers focus on how words are formed while thinking about the structure of stories.

Many struggling readers are able to predict words using fairly well-developed strategies like asking themselves what would make sense or taking their cue from the initial letter. However, as stories become more complex, the children need to check their guesses using their knowledge of word patterns and word length in combination with thinking about what would make sense. Repeated reading is a successful method for talking with struggling readers about the flexible use of their reading strategies.

Once readers have selected the passage they want to read, the teacher explains that rereading a passage is like practicing a musical instrument or soccer play. The repetition helps refine trouble-shooting strategies during reading. The teacher listens to the first oral reading and marks errors and rates fluency (1 = Slow and Word by Word; 2 = Slow and Choppy; 3 = Mostly in Phrases; 4 = Fluent). The errors and fluency rating are charted on a graph.

The teacher then encourages the child to discuss the trouble-shooting strategies he could use to correct errors. For example, the teacher could demonstrate how she might ask, "What would make sense and rhymes with 'man'?" Next, the child practices reading aloud the passage with a partner, the teacher or alone.

Afterwards, the child rereads the passage orally while the teacher marks errors and rates fluency. This second oral reading is charted in the same way as the first. The teacher and child discuss the difference between the first and second readings, focusing on the strategic reading behaviors the child used the second time.

The teacher's intervention in repeated reading activities is important, for she encourages children to integrate a variety of strategies by using prompts like, "What makes sense and starts with the letter 's'?" If a child is having a great deal of difficulty, the teacher may need to do more than prompt. It may be necessary to discuss the meaning of the selection, drawing on what the child already knows, then rephrase the prompt. If this, too, is unsuccessful, she might try echo reading — reading the lines in which the child made multiple miscues to demonstrate appropriate phrasing and intonation. Afterwards, the child reads the same line, imitating the teacher's model.

These procedures help struggling readers focus on selecting and checking cues in order to figure out words. They learn to integrate sources, asking first what would make sense and then checking the text.

RETELLING

When developing readers begin to read silently, they must be able to demonstrate their understanding of the story. Many struggling readers have trouble communicating this understanding without reading aloud directly from the text. They may have been so caught up in calling words that they forgot about the plot. Retelling is an instructional technique used to develop an oral narration of a story.

The teacher introduces a story, reminding children that stories have a beginning, middle and end, and the children read it silently. Then the teacher encourages them to talk about the story, discussing the characters, setting, problem, main episodes and resolution. If the child has trouble doing this, the teacher can interject with prompts like, "Once there was...who did...in the.... This character found that...," and so on.

By retelling the story with the help of prompts or hints from the teacher, children begin to see how they can use these prompts themselves. They think about what the author told them first (setting, characters, and problem), in the middle (the episodes), and at the end (resolution). This helps them develop and use their knowledge of story structure as they read to predict what will happen next.

STORY FRAMES

Creating story frames is another instructional technique that helps struggling readers demonstrate their understanding of stories. This particular technique, which uses a series of blanks linked by key story elements to help children focus on a particular line of thought, provides written prompts for writing a summary of narrative text.

The teacher introduces a story by inviting the children to predict what will happen. As she reads the story aloud, she stops at predetermined points to discuss the children's predictions and talk about the characters, problem and resolution. Afterwards, the teacher presents the story frame and invites the children to fill in the information. Here's an example:

The story took place in _____. The main character was _____. His problem was _____. To solve the problem, he first _____. Next, he _____. Then, he _____. Finally, he _____. This resolved the problem by _____.

Using frames like this helps struggling readers define which characters and events are important to resolving the problem presented in the story. If some readers have difficulty completing part of the frame, the teacher asks them to read orally the part of the story that applies to the blank and then asks leading questions like, "If John does get the bat, what will happen? Is this a problem for John?" If this is a persistent concern, the teacher can construct a frame that emphasizes the troublesome section. The frame might be a short one like this:

In this story, the problem starts when _____ and is resolved when _____.

This helps struggling readers focus on key aspects of story retelling. Story frames can also be used to help children generate their own stories. As students are learning how stories are formed, this technique provides them with a structure for constructing a well-formed story.

CHARACTER MAPPING

Character mapping helps struggling readers describe and remember the characters in a story by visually demonstrating their relationships and characteristics. As they read, children use the information in the text to develop their map.

The teacher introduces the main character and writes the name in the center of an overhead transparency or on the chalkboard. He then asks the children to read to find out what this character is like. They read silently to predetermined points in the story and, with the encouragement of the teacher, identify character traits and add these to the map. As they continue reading, the children and teacher return to the character map and add new characteristics as they are revealed in the story.

Character mapping helps children identify main characters and think about how their attributes influence the development of the story. When children have difficulty identifying characteristics, the teacher encourages them to read aloud sections of the story that describe the character and add this information to the map. Because a key aspect of retelling is figuring out the main characters and how they resolve conflicts, character mapping helps struggling readers with this activity. Character mapping can be extended to drawing Venn diagrams that show how characters are alike and how they're different.

Summary

The teaching strategies suggested in this chapter illustrate activities that have been used with struggling readers during the grounded phase of literacy. Most of the activities show these readers how to use textual conventions like word patterns and story structure to check their understanding. Other techniques can also be used.

. . . .

EXPANDING LITERACY

During the expanding literacy phase, developing readers extend their newly acquired knowledge of word identification and word meaning to predict the meaning of sentences as well as the overall meaning of a selection. By reading extensively, they encounter a variety of texts, sentence structures and word meanings. Instruction during this phase focuses on helping them read fluently while predicting meaning.

Difficulties

While struggling readers may display a variety of symptoms indicating that they're having trouble, the underlying problem is often a lack of fluency, both in oral reading and with developing ideas. Some struggling readers try to sound out every word individually, calling each separately and relying solely on the text to unlock meaning. The fluency of others is erratic because they don't use their knowledge of the overall text structure to check words. They, too, are caught up in the textual conventions, predicting story meaning only infrequently. Still other struggling readers fail entirely to use their own background knowledge to predict meaning. They decode individual words fluently but don't understand them or predict what their meaning might be in a story. As stories become more complex, these readers fail to use what they already know to figure out the new ideas as they encounter them.

Instructional Strategies

During this phase, instructional strategies focus on encouraging children to read fluently and make predictions about story meaning. To develop fluency, children read relatively familiar texts that allow them to predict sentence meaning readily. This often means revisiting text through readers' theater and chunking.

To help them predict story meaning, teachers encourage developing readers to use an understanding of text structure. At this stage, children begin to take a more active role in developing their own comprehension. Rather than relying on the teacher to tell them what to think about, they begin to develop their own purposes for reading. Directed reading-thinking and experience-text-relationship activities, "say something" sessions, the request technique, and literature circles help readers make this shift.

READERS' THEATER

Many struggling readers have difficulty because they're bound by the text and read word by word. Readers' theater, a technique that involves a dramatic reading of a play script where plot development is conveyed through the intonation, inflection and fluency of oral reading, helps them associate meaning with words.

Children begin by previewing the script and selecting roles. They then sit or stand at the front of the room and read their lines as expressively as possible. Afterwards, they discuss the content and how understanding this helped them read their part.

As the children interpret their character through oral reading, their reading becomes more fluent and they begin to read like they talk. This helps struggling readers convey meaning and overcome their tendency to read word by word. If a child has difficulty, the teacher can demonstrate how the character might say the lines. Initially, easy scripts need to be chosen so that children can read their part expressively without stumbling over words.

Some struggling readers don't understand that words represent thoughts. Chunking helps these children think about how words are combined to form phrases or chunks of language that mean something.

The teacher begins by explaining that reading is like thinking or talking. People talk and think in chunks of language that represent thoughts. To help readers or listeners envision a scooter, for example, we say "the red scooter" rather than "the...red...scooter."

Using a short story or poem, the teacher demonstrates his own phrasing while the child follows his model. Further, the teacher talks about the meaning of the phrases and how they enhance our ability to envision what's described. Then, the children are invited to read the story in chunks, imitating the teacher's model.

Chunking, then, helps children read in phrases or chunks that form thoughts. When someone has difficulty, the teacher models his own phrasing and encourages the child to imitate him immediately. If children can't hear their own non-fluent reading, the teacher can record one of their readings so they can begin to hear themselves.

SAY SOMETHING

The fluency of some readers is erratic because they are so caught up in textual conventions that they don't make predictions about the story. "Say something" sessions change the focus from reading to decode individual words to reading to say something. In their book, *Creating Classrooms for Authors*, Jerome Harste, Kathy Short and Carolyn Burke suggest that if children are invited to take turns saying something at intervals during the reading of a story, their ability to respond personally to literature will be enhanced.

To set the stage for "say something" sessions, the teacher and children choose an engaging text. The teacher and one of the children (or another adult, such as a teacher's aide) demonstrate how to read with a partner and express a personal response to the text as well as challenge and extend the ideas of the partner.

The children then choose partners, decide if the reading will be oral or silent, and take turns reading and saying something about what they have read.

Afterwards, the teacher guides the group to recall ideas generated during the session. These are placed on a map (character mapping is described in the preceding chapter and semantic mapping in the following chapter). The children's ideas about the theme are compared with the author's intentions. Then, the teacher engages the children in a discussion of how using this strategy helped them as they read.

This approach focuses on reading as a social process during which understanding develops through communicating ideas to others. As they share their responses to the story, the children refine their own ideas.

DIRECTED READING-THINKING ACTIVITY

Because struggling readers tend to rely on the teacher to direct activities and pose questions, they are often unaware of how to make their own predictions and monitor their own understanding. Many struggling readers are reluctant to take risks because they believe reading means getting everything right. They need to experience making predictions about a story, then confirming or rejecting these in a supportive atmosphere. This is the focus of the directed reading-thinking activity.

After choosing a book, the teacher asks the children to predict what it might be about by looking at the cover and the illustrations and reading the title. She tries to elicit as many predictions as possible.

The teacher and children then read to predetermined points where there is just enough information to confirm or reject previous predictions. Then, the teacher uses these questions to guide children to think about further predictions:

— What do think is going to happen?
— How did you figure that out?
— How is your response justified?

When the end of the book is reached, teacher and children discuss the story as a whole, talking about the content as well as their predictions.

These procedures help struggling readers predict what will happen and this, in turn, encourages fluency in reading and thinking. When struggling readers have difficulty predicting, the teacher models how she figures out her own predictions and records these along with the children's so they can evaluate the process involved in constructing meaning. These strategies help struggling readers develop an active stance as they read stories.

REQUEST TECHNIQUE

Many struggling readers have difficulty making, then analyzing, a prediction. Often, these same children may be great at generating questions, but don't seem concerned with the answers. In an article in *Journal of Reading*, Anthony Manzo suggests that the request technique, in which the teacher and children take turns asking and answering questions, can help develop comprehension.

The teacher introduces a story, paying particular attention to the title, then invites the children to read to a predetermined point. When this point is reached, the children play the role of teacher, asking questions about the story. As the teacher responds, she models using both information she found in the text and things she already knew to come up with her answers. After reading the next section, the teacher does the questioning, focusing on encouraging the children to make predictions by asking things like, "Who is the main character?" "What do you think will happen next?" and "Why do you think that?" Teacher and children continue to take turns asking and answering questions until the story is finished.

Afterwards, they discuss the selection as a whole, focusing on how their questions helped them sort out important information.

Using this technique helps children begin to develop questions about the ideas in a story and thus become more involved in thinking about its meaning. Playing the role of teacher helps struggling readers construct meaning and increases their active participation in comprehending text.

EXPERIENCE-TEXT-RELATIONSHIP

Many struggling readers have difficulty making predictions using what they already know. This is especially true of bilingual readers who may understand an experience in their own language but don't know how to represent this experience in

English. Kathryn Au suggested using a variation of the ex-perience-text-relationship — ETR — technique to help these readers develop active comprehension by showing them the relationships between their own experiences and what they're reading.

The teacher chooses a story and develops a plan for intro-ducing it to the children by relating it to what they already know. He uses broad questions to encourage them to relate their own experiences. At the end of this discussion, he guides the children to make predictions about the story using what they told him about their previous experiences.

The children read the story, stopping at critical points to discuss how what they've read so far stacks up against their predictions and relates to their own experiences.

After the reading, the teacher guides a discussion that fo-cuses on the children's overall understanding of the story. Then he directs the discussion to key aspects of the story that relate to the experiences the children have described, helping them express their understanding of the relationships be-tween their own experiences and what happened in the selec-tion.

ETR discussions proceed differently from those that often take place in typical classrooms. Initially, the teacher asks broad questions and invites all the children to talk at once to their neighbors, encouraging them to generate ideas freely in a non-judgmental atmosphere. This free-floating generation of ideas helps the children associate their own experiences with the teacher-generated questions. In bilingual classrooms, these discussions often take place in more than one language, allowing bilingual students to experiment with their own language before using English. In this way, the technique encourages children to relate their experiences to what they read in the story and finally to connect these experiences with printed language.

LITERATURE CIRCLES

Finding a purpose for reading and thinking about the ideas that might be presented in a book are difficult for struggling readers. In *Creating Classrooms for Authors*, Jerome Harste, Kathy Short and Carolyn Burke suggest that literature circles help children develop their own reasons for reading by sharing their interpretations in a discussion group. As they talk about the literature, students integrate the author's ideas and concepts with their own.

For this technique to work, it is necessary to have multiple copies of several books on hand. The teacher holds up the books and gives a short, interesting summary of each, then invites the children to choose one to read silently. Once the reading is finished, the children who have read the same book gather in a literature circle. The teacher guides then into an open-ended discussion with an invitation like, "Tell me about this book," or "Let's hear about your favorite part." At the end of the discussion time, the group decides what they will talk about the next day. At the conclusion of the discussion, group members can present their interpretation of the book to the class as a "book talk."

Because this technique helps readers develop personal reasons for reading, they become more engaged. Sensitive teachers provide a range of literature so that children can select books that are familiar to them, creating a social context that encourages individual interpretations of the text. Through sharing ideas in a peer group, students have an opportunity to define and elaborate on their own ideas.

Summary

The teaching strategies suggested in this chapter are merely examples of some of the many effective techniques that encourage children to read fluently, predicting story meaning. Most of them show children how to use their newly acquired knowledge of textual conventions to predict word and story meaning simultaneously. By using these strategies, struggling readers expand their knowledge and use of literacy.

· · · · · · · · · · · · · ·

STRATEGIC LITERACY

During this phase, the major challenge for developing readers is to take personal control of their own reading and writing. As children begin to assume control of their own literacy development, teachers concentrate on showing them how they constructed meaning rather than what they learned. Children are fascinated by their new knowledge and ability to control their thinking and, in fact, enjoy discussing how they arrived at answers. As they begin to assess the strategies they use to control their personal construction of meaning from text, they see all interactions from a personal point of view and experiment with their ideas about the world. Because they filter their view of the world through their own personal perceptions, children at this stage benefit from discussing their own learning processes.

Difficulties

Many struggling readers continually say they don't know answers, but what they are really telling the teacher is that they don't know how to get an answer. As they developed as readers, they didn't spontaneously figure out the strategies involved in the reading and writing processes and, as a result, they don't actively monitor meaning. When they're able to define their own purposes for reading and assess their progress toward reaching these goals, they become more active and in control.

Instructional Strategies

While instructional strategies may vary, at the core of each is the advancement of the reader's metacognitive attitude toward learning. Self-directed questioning has been used successfully to show them how to control their reading. Semantic mapping and a technique known as K-W-L also help children take control because they can actually see what they know before reading a passage and, afterwards, measure what they learned. Strategy instruction and reciprocal teaching are designed to show readers specific strategies, then help them use these to gain control of their reading. Readers' workshop develops this same control by encouraging children to make personal responses and exercise personal choice.

SELF-DIRECTED QUESTIONING

Struggling readers are often confused about the process of reading. They rely too much either on the text or on their own background knowledge to predict outcomes and, subsequently, fail to monitor their own understanding. Often, they hold on to inaccurate predictions even when these are contradicted by the text. These readers need to become aware that predicting, revising their predictions, and evaluating their own comprehension are active processes. Self-directed questioning is a technique that uses questions generated by the children to involve them in monitoring their own understanding.

The teacher demonstrates the active reading process by writing a series of her own thoughts about a passage on the chalkboard or an overhead transparency. These might include statements like, "I bet...," "I know that...because the text says...," or "Oops, I knew it...."

The children then read to predetermined points in a story and talk about their reading. The teacher phases in to inquire about questions they asked themselves (e.g., "What can you tell yourself about your prediction?") or to model questions she asked herself as she was reading. This encourages children to use the same strategy, asking questions, such as:

— What must I do? I must guess what's going to happen. I bet....

— What's my plan? I must use what I know. I know that....

- I wonder if it fits? I must look for hints in the text. The text says….
- Am I on the right track? I must check the text and what I know. Oops, I was wrong. That's okay, I can change my prediction. Now I bet... (or Yeah! I was right).

Afterwards, the teacher and children talk about the story and about how they constructed their responses combining what they already knew with the clues in the text. They also talk about when they changed their predictions and how often they did so. During the discussion, the teacher shares her own thought processes.

This technique helps readers not only identify how they make their predictions but also learn to assess and revise them when necessary. To do this, the teacher uses strategy-based questions like, "Does that fit your previous prediction?" "What can you tell yourself about your prediction?" "Did you use the text or your own knowledge?" "Is that important information?" and "What can you say to yourself when you change your prediction?" Because questions like these focus on monitoring comprehension rather than on coming up with right and wrong answers, they help struggling readers view reading as a process that involves actively constructing meaning. They learn that it's okay to make mistakes and revise their thinking. This is a powerful tool for passive readers who have previously regarded reading as a process that must be error-free.

K-W-L TECHNIQUE

Learning to use their own background knowledge to help decode text is often difficult for struggling readers who don't realize how much they already know and view each new reading situation as starting from scratch to learn completely unknown information. K-W-L, an abbreviation of What I *Know*, What I *Want* to Learn, What I *Learned*, is an open-ended technique set out by Donna Ogle in an article in *The Reading Teacher*. It helps readers identify what they know and what they want to learn before reading a passage, and, after reading, evaluate what they actually did learn. It's used to direct children's reading in and learning from content-area texts and helps develop their perception of reading as an active process.

Beforehand, the teacher prepares worksheets containing three columns headed K — What I Know, W — What I Want to Learn and L — What I Learned. Once a topic is selected, he works with the children to brainstorm ideas about it and writes these on the chalkboard or chart paper. Then, the children write what they know under the K (What I Know) column on their own worksheet. Together, the teacher and children categorize the items in the K column and the children generate questions they would like answered about the topic, writing these in the W (What I Want to Learn) column.

As children read the text — or various texts — silently, they add new questions to the W (What I Want to Learn) column and information to the L (What I Learned) column. After reading, they complete the L column, then work with the teacher to review the first two columns, tying together what they already knew and the questions they had with what they learned.

This technique helps children visualize concretely what they already know, the questions they have, and what they learned from text. In the process, they learn to define their own goals and assess what they're learning.

SEMANTIC MAPPING

Many struggling readers have difficulty thinking about what new words mean. They passively read these words as if this in itself will create understanding. They need to learn to use what they already know about the textual information as they read. Semantic mapping develops word meaning by visually representing the relationship between a key word and its attributes or related concepts.

The teacher begins by presenting one or two key words in the center of an overhead transparency or the chalkboard. The students brainstorm to come up with attributes of and concepts related to this word while the teacher writes what they say in a pattern resembling the spokes of a wheel. The diagram on the following page illustrates what this might look like.

The children then read the text silently, expanding their understanding of the key words or concepts. Afterwards, they return with the teacher to the semantic map and add the newly learned information. Often, this means constructing a new

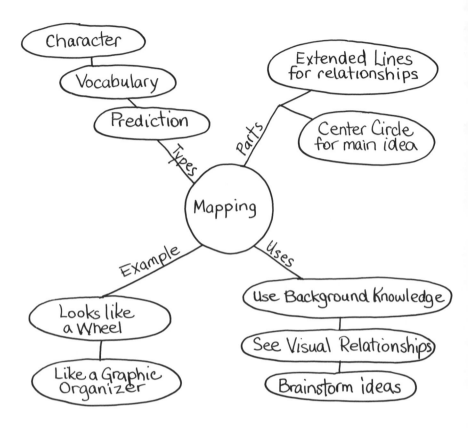

map so the conceptual relationships between the key word and its attributes and related concepts are clearly delineated.

Semantic mapping helps struggling readers use what they already know as they read, then expand what they know after they read. This is important because familiarity with vocabulary is important to understanding information in content subjects. As they compare what they put on the map before and after reading, struggling readers can readily evaluate what they learned about the new concepts.

STRATEGY INSTRUCTION

Because struggling readers are often unaware of the strategies proficient readers use to solve problems as they read, they passively read text without constructing meaning. To help them, teachers can explain, demonstrate and coach them in using strategies.

The teacher begins by explaining what strategic reading is and how the targeted strategies fit into the reading process. In other words, he sets goals emphasizing use of a particular strategy, such as predicting. Then he explains when and where he might use this strategy, demonstrating his own internal thought processes as he proceeds through the steps involved in using it.

Then, as children read, the teacher actively coaches them as they think aloud. This helps them modify and elaborate on their strategies. The teacher provides feedback, phasing in to coach thinking and phasing out to encourage children to use strategies independently. This helps youngsters focus on how they got an answer as well as what they understood. Afterwards, the teacher encourages the children to think and talk about how using the strategies contributed to their successful comprehension of the passage.

This technique explains the process of reading to children and, as teachers coach them to think, helps struggling readers take control of their own literacy.

RECIPROCAL TEACHING

Reciprocal teaching, a technique developed by Annemarie Palinscar and Ann Brown, encourages children to take the role of teacher and pose questions, ask for clarification, make predictions and construct summaries as they lead a discussion.

Working with a small group, the teacher selects a passage and demonstrates the steps involved in the process.

— Generate a good question or two.
— Review troublesome aspects of the passage, noting new vocabulary and the organization of the text.
— Formulate a summary, including main ideas and details.
— Predict what the author will discuss next.

The children then take turns leading the discussion group using the steps modeled by the teacher, who joins the group and assists them when necessary by asking leading questions and demonstrating strategies like, "That was a good summary. I would summarize by including...because it is an important idea."

Later, as the children use the strategies independently, the teacher continues to participate in the group but phases out her support. Inviting struggling readers to lead the discussion helps them begin to identify reasons for summarizing and generating questions. As they do so, they become active, rather than passive, learners.

READERS' WORKSHOP

Some struggling readers, who depend on the teacher to tell them what to look for and how to read, have trouble developing their own reasons for reading. These readers need time to read and write for their own purposes. Readers' workshop, a technique developed by Nancie Atwell, immerses children for several days in stories they have selected themselves. The program has several elements — mini-lessons, sustained silent reading and dialogue response journals.

For an extended period every day, children read materials they have selected themselves, keeping response journals in which they write their thoughts, feelings, questions and concerns about the book. The teacher responds in writing to the journal entries, coaching the children to think about the story and probing their thinking. For example, she might write, "I have a clear picture of the main character, but I don't understand the conflict. Can you tell me more?" In this way, she encourages the children to construct meaning. At appropriate moments, based on her perception of the children's needs, the teacher conducts mini-lessons to demonstrate thinking processes she uses herself when reading. For example, she might talk aloud about a character's problem and how she thinks it might be solved. Eventually, the children begin to write entries expressing opinions based on the text and their personal knowledge.

Readers' workshops provide an excellent setting for the teacher to demonstrate how to think about literature. The dialogue journals and mini-lessons help struggling readers take control of their reading by encouraging them to read actively for individual purposes.

Summary

The strategies suggested in this chapter represent only a few of the techniques that can be used to help develop strategic literacy. They encourage children to take control of and evaluate their own reading strategies.

. . . .

REFLECTIVE LITERACY

During this phase, readers elaborate on their understanding of ideas from a variety of sources. They develop their understanding that some things are more important than others and select key ideas across several pieces of literature in order to summarize and remember critical information. They use these strategies to justify their own point of view and distinguish it from that of the author and other adults and children.

Reflective literacy means just what it says. Readers in this phase begin to evaluate and refine their thinking by writing about and reflecting on their ideas as they discuss and review their own thoughts and writing with the teacher and other children.

Difficulties

Often the children who experience difficulty during this phase of literacy are those who try to remember everything as if it were new information. They don't use their previous knowledge of a topic to consolidate information, define its importance, and elaborate on categories of information. They also view literacy events in isolation rather than looking for patterns among ideas.

Instructional Strategies

Discussion and writing are critical to enhancing reflective thinking because these activities help children elaborate on and modify their thinking as they verbalize and write about their ideas. Likewise, researching and writing about ideas encourage children to expand their understanding. Strategies such as learning logs and dialogue journals help them reflect on their learning. Creating graphic organizers helps them understand relationships among concepts while generating questions develops their ability to evaluate the importance of information.

LEARNING LOGS

Struggling readers sometimes become so caught up in reading and writing that they don't reflect on and evaluate their own learning. This inhibits their ability to assess their own literacy and keeps them dependent on the teacher. In *Creating Classrooms for Authors*, Jerome Harste, Kathy Short and Carolyn Burke suggest that teachers can use learning logs in a variety of content areas to help readers move towards independent, reflective thinking. Keeping logs encourages children to think and write about their learning on a daily basis. While they can write about content or processes, it is important that they review their logs as units of study wind up.

Each child will need a notebook to use as a personal learning log. As they engage in learning activities, they make entries in their logs by writing about something they're learning. These logs can be brought to discussion groups where the information they contain can be used to back up children's opinions and ideas.

Learning logs can be used in many classroom situations. For example, literature logs can be used for writing about novels or poems while science logs can be devoted to writing about experiments or passages in textbooks. Children can keep observation logs of science activities, such as growing plants, or of social science events, such as coverage of a news item. Teachers respond to the children's log entries by encouraging them to think about how ideas relate. They might, for example, write, "I liked the observations you made, but did you ever think about how...and...relate to each other?"

This approach, developed by Carol Santa, Susan Dailey and Marilyn Nelson, engages children in reflective thinking by asking them to write opinions backed up by evidence found in a reading selection.

The teacher introduces a selection from a specific content area and invites children to think about opinions they might have about the characters or concepts presented in the passage.

After the children read the selection silently, the teacher explains the opinion-proof guide either on the chalkboard or with a handout. The guide is a sheet of paper divided into two columns. In the left column, headed Opinion, children write their opinions about characters or concepts. For example, if the passage is about amending the Constitution, the children might set out their opinion about a particular proposal. In the right column, headed Proof, children record information that justifies their opinion. While this can be drawn from their own background knowledge, it should also include information from the text. If necessary, the teacher can help them select supporting information.

After the opinion-proof guide is completed, the children use it as the basis for writing an essay that is then shared with a partner or group.

The opinion-proof approach encourages children to reflect on their ideas before a discussion takes place. Recording their thoughts helps them expand their ideas by combining information found in the text with their personal background knowledge. In this way, they learn to explain their thinking. During the follow-up discussion, they often revise their thinking, reflecting on what they wrote and how the group responded to their ideas.

GRAPHIC ORGANIZER

Some struggling readers have difficulty organizing a mass of new information into categories and relationships. Instead of trying to remember every new fact as an unrelated piece of information, these students need help organizing the new information into categories and relating it to their background knowledge. Graphic organizers provide a visual representation of the main concepts in a content area. By arranging the key words in a chapter, for example, the teacher and children develop an idea framework for relating unfamiliar vocabulary and concepts.

The teacher presents the graphic organizer on the chalkboard or an overhead transparency. As she does so, she explains the relationships she is showing. Students, too, are encouraged to explain how they think the information is related. After reading a selection, children then generate their own graphic organizers.

Graphic organizers are flexible and can follow a number of patterns:

- A network tree. This places the main concepts at the top of a page, then shows subordinate information linked to the main concept in hierarchical fashion. It might be used to show, for example, the branches of government.
- Cycle frame. This shows critical events that repeat themselves in a circular chain. It might be used to show, for example, the water cycle or metamorphosis.

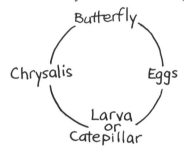

- Continuum. This is often used in history and mathematics to show a sequence of events or degree of measurement.
- Venn diagram. This can be used to show how concepts are interrelated as well as how they are discrete. For example, Venn diagrams that analyze main characters from different books help children see how they are alike and how they are different.

Graphic organizers help struggling readers consolidate information and organize and relate important concepts. Teachers can help children identify major headings and factual relationships by asking questions like, "Is that important information?" "Where should it go on the graphic?" and "How does it relate to the other information?"

Many struggling readers have difficulty identifying important information when reading textbooks or non-fiction materials. Encouraging them to generate their own questions by thinking about the information they should remember helps them define what's important.

Using a short paragraph as an example, the teacher demonstrates how he makes up questions, stressing that the questions are about important information in the text. Then he invites the children to read a selection silently and, afterwards, make up questions of their own. To follow up, the teacher and children share their questions and the teacher provides feedback about their importance.

The same technique can also help children sort out important information in a novel. If the questions are written on cards and filed in a box, other children who read the same book can answer them in the form of a book report.

Developing questions in this way helps struggling readers define important information.

Summary

The teaching strategies suggested in this chapter represent only a few of the activities that can enhance reflective thinking. They depend on children using writing a means of reflecting on their understanding and then sharing that writing in a discussion group. This sharing encourages further reflection and rewriting.

ASSESSING LITERACY

As our view of literacy changes, so too do the techniques we use to assess this complex, dynamic process. No longer is the static measurement of skill mastery considered an adequate evaluation of literacy. When literacy is viewed as an active process of constructing meaning, in which the reader's application of skills and strategies varies with the demands of the reading situation, the assessment techniques we use must reflect this. Not only do they need to be grounded in the interactive view of literacy, but they also need to focus on what readers can already do. Assessment must be continuous, using a variety of process-oriented techniques that reflect the changing nature of literacy and represent literacy development over time.

Rethinking Assessment

When selecting and creating process-oriented assessment techniques, teachers need new criteria for judging whether they are appropriate. Evaluating whether a technique is authentic, instructionally valid and used consistently can help guide the selection process.

Is the assessment activity authentic?

Assessment tools used in classrooms must replicate real-life situations. For example, in real life, people often retell stories they have read. This means that evaluating children's retelling of stories is an authentic form of assessment. It shows them both what they can already do and where they need to improve, thus enhancing their ability to interact with the world at large. On the other hand, measuring mastery of activities that bear no resemblance to real-life situations, such as skill-and-drill exercises, is not an authentic assessment technique.

Is the assessment activity instructionally valid?

Sometimes there is a need to evaluate behaviors specific to the task of acquiring literacy. These measures provide evidence of how children are learning and thinking about a particular task or topic discussed in the classroom. This can be tricky, because the instruction must be also be valid. If the instruction focuses on a particular task that will lead to authentic literacy, then the measure is said to be instructionally valid. For instance, fluent oral reading in itself is not an authentic literacy activity because few people regularly read orally in public. However, fluent reading indicates that a child has integrated the tasks of processing both print and meaning, and this is an authentic literacy task.

Does the assessment format allow teachers to interpret children's responses consistently?

The assessment formats teachers choose help them reflect on how children are developing as literate individuals. As we observe children in authentic and instructionally valid activities, we interpret the data in light of our own understanding of literacy development and the interactive view of literacy. The format we use helps us judge children's behavior in a consistent manner. For example, every time a teacher uses a checksheet to evaluate a child's retelling of a story, she must be consistent in her judgments about what counts.

Equally important is the teacher's interpretation of the child's responses in light of her knowledge of literate behaviors. We must be careful not to make broad generalizations about literacy based on an assessment technique designed for a specific purpose. For example, an assessment tool that measures a child's knowledge of story structure, a single aspect of comprehension, should not be used as a basis for evaluating the child's literacy development in general.

Teachers need to select assessment tools that are authentic and instructionally valid and use them consistently. We need to remember that any assessment technique provides only a snapshot of literacy development at a particular moment. It never really captures the variety of situations that readers encounter. However, by using a variety of assessment tools in the classroom, an authentic evaluation of a student's continuing literacy development can be achieved.

This chapter suggests a variety of tools that can be used to measure literacy development during particular phases. However, their authenticity and instructional validity are not necessarily limited to a particular phase. Many can be used effectively during various stages of development. For example, because the self-assessment technique matches the developmental task of controlling learning, it appears in the section titled Strategic Literacy. However, because many children benefit from conducting self-assessments throughout their entire literacy development, its usefulness is not limited to this phase.

Emergent Literacy

During the emergent phase, readers predict the words in books based on their own knowledge and the context of the literacy event. For this reason, the tools used during this phase need to be situated within an environment in which children are making sense of print. Interviews that measure children's awareness of print and running records, a technique that evaluates children's reading miscues, are authentic methods of assessing children's literacy and provide valuable information that can guide instruction.

PRINT AWARENESS INTERVIEW

While various procedures have been developed for assessing young children's awareness of print, the most natural technique involves simply handing them a book — or language experience story — and asking questions. Describing their responses helps teachers evaluate how young children are developing a working knowledge of print.

— Hand a child a book or story and ask where he will begin reading. Does he know that the story begins where the print begins?

— Ask where he will go next. Does he know that the left page comes before the right? That readers move from the top to the bottom of the page? That he should begin at the left and read along the line to the right, then return to the left margin of the next line?
— Read a line of the story and ask the child to repeat it. Does he know when he read too many or too few words?
— Ask him to point to a word. Does he know what a word is?
— Ask him to point to a letter and name it. Does he understand what a letter is? Can he name the letters?

RUNNING RECORDS

Teachers constantly listen to children read, deciding whether they're ready to progress to more difficult material. This simple technique was, however, obscured for a time by an overemphasis on skill development. Running records, developed by Marie Clay, are powerful tools for assessing progress and the match between reader and text.

An informal variation on Clay's system is to invite a child to read aloud a selection (about 50-100 words) and count the number of miscues. For a story to be suitable for instruction, the child should not miss more than one word in 10. If the miscue rate is higher than this, the text is too difficult and the teacher needs to find another that is less challenging.

This system also provides insights into the cuing system the child uses. Teachers can record the exact miscue and compare it to the original text, asking these questions:

— Does the word make sense?
— Does it fit grammatically in the sentence?
— Does the replacement word start with the same letter(s)?
— Does the child try to sound out the word?

As teachers listen to children read, they look for a pattern of miscues over time. Evaluating the cue system helps teachers match instruction to what children can already do and analyzing the pattern of miscues provides insights into the troubleshooting strategies children use when reading breaks down.

Because readers use the text, both single words and story structure, to predict words and story meaning during the grounded literacy phase, assessment techniques need to reflect their growing understanding of print and story structure. While various procedures for assessing children's knowledge of the relationship between sounds and symbols have been developed, the most natural of these involves evaluating how the child uses this system when writing. Likewise, a natural technique for evaluating comprehension is to assess the child's retelling of a story.

Spelling features assessment is designed to evaluate the child's knowledge of the relationship between sounds and symbols while story structure assessment evaluates comprehension. Both these tools provide valuable information about how young children cope with the conventions of print. To save time, the teacher can use the same written story summary to measure both spelling (graphophonic) awareness and story structure completeness. If these summaries are collected over the course of the school year, they provide a concrete indication of how children's literacy development is progressing.

SPELLING FEATURES ASSESSMENT

To place the assessment of phonics knowledge in context, teachers can examine samples of children's writing, which reveals their memory for sounds in words and how these are combined to form words.

The teacher selects a writing sample and scores each word according the following scale. In each category, there is a list of the characteristics of the stage. If the student's spelling exhibits most of the characteristics, it receives the score indicated.

Pre-Sounding-Out Stage
(Score 0 for each word in this category)

— Letter forms represent a message.
— No sound-symbol relationship exhibited.
— Writes and repeats known letters fairly accurately (may have many upper-case letters).

Early Sounding-Out Stage
(Score 1 for each word in this category)

- Whole words are represented by one or more letters.
- This letter (or letters) represents some of the sounds in words, but not all.
- Letter-naming strategy is limited and random.

Sounding-Out Stage
(Score 2 for each word in this category)

- Writes a letter for more than half the sounds in the word.
- Represents sounds with a letter name (letter-naming strategy is prevalent and ordered).
- Spaces appear between most words.

Transitional Stage
(Score 3 for each word in this category)

- Letter-sound relationships based on standard spelling.
- Conventional rules are used appropriately, but not correctly (e.g., "littel" for "little").
- Reverses some letters in words.

Correct Spelling
(Score 4 for each word in this category)

- Uses conventional spelling.
- Entire word spelled correctly.

The teacher adds together the scores, then finds the average by dividing the total score by the total number of words in the sample. This average helps him assess readers according to their stage of spelling (graphophonic) development. For example, if a child's average is 2.5, the teacher can indicate that she is in the sounding-out stage.

While scoring a passage using a spelling features list helps teachers analyze a child's spelling and phonics awareness, it is the evaluation process that is important rather than the score. The evaluation helps teachers identify what children can already do and monitor their developing graphophonic knowledge.

A simple, authentic tool for assessing silent reading comprehension is to evaluate a child's retelling of a story. As children retell a story orally, the teacher evaluates whether the retelling includes the setting, characters, problem, events and resolution. The same method can be used with a written summary.

The following simple format provides a quantitative score for a retelling. While it may sometimes be necessary for the teacher to provide prompts, this should be done sparingly. The idea is to evaluate each child's ability to retell the story without assistance.

Before starting, the teacher needs to analyze the story to identify the setting, problem, plot episodes and resolution. As a child retells the story, the teacher records a score for each category using the following guide.

Story Structure Assessment Rating Guide

Setting   Rating (0-4)____

4 Includes an introduction, names of main character and other characters, description of important places and times.
3 Includes main character and some other characters, brief description of place and time.
2 Includes main character and briefly states times or place.
1 Includes only one element, such as place or names of minor characters.
0 Does not include any information related to setting.

Problem   Rating (0-4)____

4 Includes an elaboration of the main character's primary goal or problem to be solved, including motive or theme of story. This also includes the event that sets up the problem in the story.
3 Includes primary problem main character needs to solve.
2 Includes only a sketchy idea of the problem.
1 Includes an unrelated problem.
0 Does not include problem.

Events   Rating (0-4)____

4 Includes key events or plot episodes that lead to resolution. Most events or episodes mentioned are related to attempts to solve the problem, a consequence of this action and the characters' reaction to the situation.
3 Includes some key events and some of these relate to attempts to solve the problem, a consequence of this action and the characters' reaction to the situation.
2 Includes some key events but does not elaborate on them.
1 Includes only a few unnrelated events.
0 Does not include any key events.

Resolution   Rating (0-4)____

4 Ends the story so there is a sense of sequence and describes how the problem was resolved and the goal attained.
3 Ends the story so there is a sense of sequence and briefly tells how the problem was resolved.
2 Ends the story so there is a sense of sequence, but does not tell how the problem was resolved.
1 Ends the story abruptly.
0 Stops in the middle of the story.

TOTAL SCORE   ____

Expanding Literacy

During this phase, children read widely to develop their ability to read fluently with comprehension. Struggling readers, too, need to read widely so they can independently use the strategies learned during the first two phases of development. To help them, teachers need to match instruction to the children's strategies, evaluating their reading behavior and book selections.

ASSESSMENT DURING LESSONS

When assessing during a lesson, the teacher watches readers' behaviors and evaluates their responses. For example, when using directed reading-thinking activities, the teacher can use the following guide to create an anecdotal record of a child's responses.

DRTA Evaluation
(Rate from 1 to 4: 4 indicates almost always, 1 indicates almost never.)

Predictions

• Makes predictions readily ___
• Uses previous experiences ___
• Uses textual information ___

Monitoring

• Checks predictions ___
• Revises predictions when necessary ___
• Justifies responses ___
• Uses previous experiences ___
• Uses text examples ___
• Rereads when necessary ___

Extension

• Can expand responses ___
• Integrates both the text and previous knowledge ___
• Compares this story with others ___

Summarizing

• Important information included ___
• Critical inferences made ___
• Response well-formed ___

For any lesson framework, teachers can construct a checklist to evaluate children's responses during the lesson. When using the request technique, for example, a similar form can be used, deleting the section titled Monitoring and adding an element dealing with questions and answers. It might include statement such as, Asks literal questions, Asks for a prediction, and Answers prediction questions. While checklists like this can be used during every phase of literacy development, they are particularly useful during the expanding literacy stage because the children's engagement in a literacy activity needn't stop to allow the teacher to test.

Equally important during this phase is the measurement of fluent oral reading. Often teachers worry unnecessarily about children's fluency during the grounded stage when, because the major task is to master the patterns of words and text, students need to read more slowly. Developing and assessing fluency becomes more important during the expanding literacy phase when assessment needs to measure whether children are spontaneously linking what words look like with what they mean in the context of the passage.

To do this, the teacher can ask children to read a paragraph aloud and rate the reading. In my own work at the reading clinic at Eastern Montana College, I've found that students and teachers can successfully rate fluency using a three point scale.

Fluency Scale

— Non-fluent reading, marked by word-by-word reading, numerous pauses, sound-outs, repetitions and/or lack of intonation and expression.

— Reading is somewhat fluent and has one of two patterns: a) Slow and erratic reading in two- and three-word phrases; intonation appears choppy because of pauses to sound out or repeat words.
b) Reasonable pace but improper phrasing and intonation.

— Fluent reading with longer phrases and good expression and intonation. Repetitions are to correct errors in phrasing or expression.

Fluent readers receive a score of three while developing readers would receive a score of two. Struggling readers who receive a score of one need more opportunities to read easy selections and hear the teacher's model.

OBSERVING BOOK SELECTIONS

During the expanding literacy phase, one measure of children's progress towards more fluent reading is the number and kinds of books they select to read independently. Teachers, parents and librarians can work together to summarize information about children's book selection habits. For example, some items on an observation record might include:

Book Selection Checklist

- Number of books checked out ___
- Number of books read ___

Rate the following on a scale of 1 to 4, with 4 meaning almost always and 1 meaning almost never.

- Discussed books with friends ___
- Was engaged reading books for an extended time ___

Strategic Literacy

As children begin to control their own literacy development, teachers need to focus on *how* they construct meaning rather than on what they learn. Students are fascinated by their new knowledge and the realization that they can control their own thinking and, in fact, enjoy discussing how they arrived at answers. Because an important factor in developing control is learning to evaluate oneself, children's ability to assess their own literacy development becomes critical during this phase and it's a good idea to involve them in assessment activities.

QUALITATIVE ASSESSMENT OF RETELLINGS

While there is a continued emphasis on summarizing narrative and expository passages during this phase, evaluation focuses on the children's use of strategies to link text and background knowledge, monitor comprehension, define purposes and expand meaning.

Judy Mitchell of the University of Arizona and Pi Irwin of the Tucson Unified School District have worked extensively with the following assessment technique, which focuses on how comprehension is occurring by measuring how children summarized the story rather than what they said. The first four items indicate the reader's comprehension of textual information while the next four indicate metacognitive awareness, strategy use, and involvement with the text. The final four items indicate facility with language and language development. These items can be rated on a scale from 1 to 4 with 4 meaning a high degree and 1 meaning none.

Process Evaluation of Retellings

The retelling:

- includes information directly stated in the text.
- includes information inferred directly or indirectly from the text.
- includes what is important to remember from the text.
- provides relevant content and concepts.
- indicates reader's attempt to connect background knowledge to text information.
- indicates reader's attempt to make summary statements or generalizations based on text that can be applied to the real world.
- indicates highly individualistic and creative impressions of or reactions to the text.
- indicates the reader's affective involvement with the text.
- demonstrates appropriate use of language (vocabulary, sentence structure, language conventions).
- indicates reader's ability to organize or compose the retelling.
- demonstrates the reader's sense of audience or purpose.
- indicates the reader's control of the mechanics of speaking or writing.

SELF-ASSESSMENT

Because self-assessment asks children to conduct an internal dialogue about their reading strategies, this technique increases their involvement in their own learning. In a presentation to the annual convention of the International Reading Association, Susan Glazer suggested that children need a new language to talk about their own learning. This language would focus on "I" statements as youngsters talk about how they are comprehending and controlling their own literacy. Teachers need to offer children consistent evaluation tools, such as checklists related to specific literacy tasks like story structure summaries, questionnaires focusing on strategies, and statements related to what they know and learned.

It's a good idea to invite children to assess themselves both before and after completing a task. For example, the K-W-L technique (where children write what they know in one column and what they learned in another) lends itself nicely to self-assessment. The teacher can draw attention to the information the student has learned through reading.

In some content-area classrooms, teachers are experimenting with open-ended questions to focus self-evaluation. They ask the children to write and respond to questions like these:

— What did I learn about sharing my ideas?
— What did I learn about putting my ideas together?
— What did I learn about the topic?

DISCUSSION GROUP ASSESSMENTS

Another way to help students reflect on their own development is to invite group members to evaluate their learning as a group. This helps students look back on how they shared their knowledge and think about how their knowledge is developing. For example, individual members of a discussion group might complete the following open-ended statements:

— Something everyone in the group learned was...
— Each person learned something different. Some of the things we learned were...
— As a group, we had new questions. They were...

An activity like this helps children develop a broader perspective on their own literacy development. As they think about their own literacy and evaluate what others are learning, they refine their thinking about literacy development in general.

Reflective Literacy

During this stage, the same assessment techniques applied during other phases can be used — but in a different way. As they think about their own literacy, children — and the teacher — need to use various tools to assess their continuing development. Portfolios of children's writing about their reading are integral to assessment during this stage.

As children increasingly analyze their own development and how they synthesize and organize information, their reflective literacy is extended.

Portfolios contain multiple samples of classroom work completed over an extended period. Because the work samples emerge out of classroom literacy events, they exist in context. Teaching and learning do not stop in order to test; rather, assessment becomes integral to learning. Because it might include multiple drafts of a particular piece, a portfolio can demonstrate the process of learning as well as the content learned.

The reflective process involved in choosing what is included in the portfolio is the most authentic evidence of a child's learning. To each selection, children attach a paragraph explaining why it was included. When choosing what to include in their portfolios, children must reflect on their own literacy development, evaluate their learning and set new goals for themselves. Thus, portfolios are integrated into the curriculum, serving as a mirror of each child's learning.

JOURNAL ASSESSMENT

A written journal is an excellent avenue for encouraging children to reflect on how and what they are learning. Both the children and teacher can reread journal entries using a checklist to evaluate how comprehension is progressing. The following items can be rated with a Yes or No or on a graduated scale of 1 to 4.

Journal Checklist

Responses:

- are scant — single ideas and not the main one.
- become longer and more detailed over time.
- are emotional reactions.
- explain the story.
- show reasoning about the story.
- include descriptions of how comprehension is happening (e.g., describes strategies).
- show reflective development of an idea or concept.

Teacher as Evaluator

Changes in our view of literacy have led not only to the use of assessment techniques that are authentic and instructionally valid but also to the realization that evaluation must be carried out by teachers and students, not by tests. As we spend time listening to children, we get to know them in a personal way. We can deepen our knowledge about individual children's attitudes towards literacy by conducting interviews to probe this. Questions asked during these interviews might include:

— What is reading?
— What is writing?
— Who is a good reader that you know?
— What makes him or her a good reader?
— Do you think you're a good reader? Why?
— If some friends were having trouble reading, how could you help them?
— When you're reading and come to something you don't know, what do you do?

Listening to the children helps teachers evaluate their own beliefs about literacy and the effect of these beliefs on the children's literacy development. This, in turn, helps us think about our instructional decisions and come to view these as part of the continuing assessment that happens in the classroom.

Summary

The assessment techniques outlined in this chapter can help teachers become more reflective as we observe children learning and analyze the instructional situation. Then, we interpret the data we're collecting, giving it meaning by judging the children's behavior against our understanding of literacy development. Based on this judgment, we assess children's level of engagement in the interactive reading process and make instructional decisions.

. . . .

WORKING TOGETHER

An unfortunate by-product of our technological society has been the separation, rather than the collaboration, of instructional efforts. Rather than sharing expertise with one another, teachers often view themselves as marooned alone on their classroom islands. This is particularly unfortunate for struggling readers because they, above all others, need the shared expertise of the professionals within a school. Often, special programs designed for children who are experiencing reading difficulty decrease rather than increase their chances of developing literate behaviors. In addition, studies have shown that struggling readers actually receive a lower quantity and quality of instruction than their more proficient counterparts. It is time to devise new frameworks that will pull together professional and community resources to provide a cohesive program for these readers.

Parents as Partners

Family literacy plays an integral role in shaping children's attitudes towards literacy. When children interact in literacy activities with adults and peers and when adults serve as positive models for literacy behaviors, the growth of literacy is fostered. Thus, in homes where few family interactions center around print, children do not build a background of experiences that enables them to respond to literacy naturally.

In addition, parents who have experienced stressful learning situations themselves, often find it difficult to assist struggling readers. Their child's struggle brings to the surface many of the negative emotional responses and inappropriate behaviors they themselves developed in school.

There are, however, ways to work with parents to help them view literacy in a new light and work successfully with their children. In an article in *Reading Research Quarterly*, Lynda Mudre and Sandra McCormick report that parents — or significant others — have been shown how to use prompts that focus on meaning, such as "Does that make sense?" and "Read that again and see if it makes sense," while listening to their children read. They received guidance in waiting before prompting and in what to say when their child faltered. In addition, they were given suggestions for when and how to provide support and encouragement.

Staff Review Process

Another tactic for sharing expertise is the staff review process. This involves a chairperson, the child's classroom teacher and a recording secretary who meet as a group to share their perspectives on a specific reader. The chairperson and the classroom teacher prepare questions and data. At the meeting, the classroom teacher presents the collected data, which includes information about the child's strengths, interests, behaviors, beliefs about literacy, relationships with others, and greatest needs. The group reviews the data and suggests possible strategies, building on what the child can already do. This process takes advantage of the expertise of the regular classroom teacher to solve problems. Decisions about children are based on data from extended observations within the context of the actual classroom.

Congruence Model

Another model that relies on the sharing of expertise is the congruence model. In their essay in *Beyond Separate Education*, Richard Allington and Anne McGill-Franzen suggest that school personnel combine their instructional practices into a unified plan for struggling readers. Like the staff review process, groups of teachers consider a child's program in a variety of instructional situations. These teachers develop a body of shared knowledge about the children, their reading instruction, the core curriculum and themselves. Even though the school's program may need to be adapted to help struggling readers, it remains congruent with the program of instruction for all children in the school.

Collaborative Education Model

Struggling readers need to use active reading and thinking strategies alongside their peers. If this happens in the regular classroom, these readers have appropriate role models and a chance to share their own thinking. Rather than offering a watered-down curriculum in a special classroom, the collaborative education model involves the reading specialist in supporting the efforts of struggling readers in the regular classroom. This means that the specialist and the classroom teacher work together, sharing their expertise within the same classroom to provide high-quality instruction for every child. Special study classes before and after school are open to all students, rather than only to those labeled as having difficulty. With this approach, struggling readers are constantly challenged by the thinking of more proficient readers.

Summary

This chapter suggests that schools and communities share their expertise. Strategies for doing so can include welcoming parents as partners in their children's education and developing coherence among programs and collaboration among staff and community members. All the suggestions require teachers and administrators to look closely at how instruction affects struggling readers.

. . . .

A FINAL LOOK

This book has explained how reading difficulties can be attributed to a failure in the interaction between readers and their instructional environment, rather than solely to the shortcomings of a particular child. We know that many struggling readers often spend less time reading and receive less reading instruction than their more proficient counterparts. The result is that they become disenchanted with school, barely scraping through. Their weak reading strategies inhibit not only their learning in school but also their ability to make a smooth transition from school to productive lives.

In this book, we've looked at how:

— the instructional program influences reading behaviors both positively and negatively at each juncture of a child's academic career. These programs need to build on the shared expertise of professionals in the school and the community.
— teachers' instructional decisions and behaviors have a powerful influence on children's learning. Instruction needs to focus on helping children construct meaning, always emphasizing making sense out of stories and information.

This interactive view of literacy has tremendous implications for teachers. A few of these are:

Instructional adjustments must become the rule rather than the exception.

Many teachers find it hard to change their plans — even when it's obvious that what they're doing isn't working. What struggling readers need most is sensitive teachers who can adapt their instruction on the spot, immediately using what the children can already do to create alternative learning situations. Our attitude, words and encouragement strategies communicate that everyone is capable of learning.

Instructional decisions must be based on continuing, authentic assessment of children's progress.

As teachers become evaluators, we must continually assess how struggling readers are learning. It is necessary for us to return to the model of active literacy, evaluating how the children use multiple sources of information to predict, check their predictions and expand both their content knowledge and strategy options and their interpretations of the context of literacy. True and fair assessment of children's progress emerges from observations made during instruction.

Teachers must become reflective.

As we intuitively plan activities and make adjustments, we must step back from the hectic instructional day and ask ourselves, Why did I change and what did I accomplish with the change? In other words, we need to take time to make sense of our instructional decisions. As we solve these complex instructional problems, we become creators of curriculum.

We must become researchers in our own classrooms.

As we adjust our plans and assess literacy, we need to synthesize our observations about struggling readers and the instructional alternatives we create. This information becomes the research upon which to build new curriculum.

As teachers, we must ourselves become powerful models of literate behaviors.

We must read and write for our own individual purposes in the classroom. We must share our secrets about literacy and about children. As we solve complex instructional problems, we need to share our problem-solving strategies with students, parents, other teachers and administrators.

We must set sail from our classroom island to the mainland of collaborative instructional programs.

In this way, struggling readers can immerse themselves in real reading situations where they can share their interpretations with their peers.

As we work with struggling readers, we must not lose sight of the fact that, at one time, these children actively sought meaning within a literacy community. At some point in their academic careers, however, there was a mismatch between the instruction they received and their own unique strategies for constructing meaning. They experienced failure and began to struggle to make sense of what they were reading. Thereafter, these readers struggled daily to make sense, often doubting themselves and shifting blame to whomever and whatever they could in order to maintain their sense of self-worth.

We must open our minds and hearts to these children so they can feel significant in our classrooms and our lives. We must accept the legitimacy of the unique strategies they use and acknowledge that their struggle is real. But, in our compassion, we must not hook into their failure. We must create the very best instructional opportunities, giving them far more than our sympathy. We need to create instructional situations that begin with what they can already do, guiding them to expand their strategy resources. We need to listen to and support these readers as they discuss the strategies they're using and how their attempts to make sense are working. We need to rejoice with them in their successes and help them celebrate their own literacy.

I hope this book helps you create instructional opportunities to transform the struggling readers in your care into readers who can again make sense of the literacy events in their lives.

. . . .

BIBLIOGRAPHY

Allington, R.L. "Oral Reading." In *Handbook of Reading Research*. (P.D. Pearson, Ed.). New York: Longman, 1984.

Allington, R.L. & A. McGill-Franzen, "Different Programs, Indifferent Instruction." In *Beyond Separate Education*. (D. Lispsky & A. Gartner, Eds.) Baltimore, Maryland: Paul H. Brooks, 1989.

Anderson, R.C., E.H. Hiebert, J.A. Scott & I.A.G. Wilkinson. *Becoming a Nation of Readers*. Washington, D.C.: National Institute of Education, 1985.

Atwell, N.M. *In the Middle: Writing, Reading and Learning with Adolescents*. Upper Montclair, New Jersey: Boynton/Cook, 1987.

Au, K. "Using the Experience-Text-Relationship Method with Minority Children." In *The Reading Teacher*. Vol. 32, No. 6 (1979).

Baker, L., & A. Brown. "Metacognitive Skills and Reading." In *Handbook of Reading Research*. (P.D. Pearson, Ed.). New York: Longman, 1984.

Bristow, P.S. "Are Poor Readers Passive Readers? Some Evidence, Possible Explanations, and Potential Solutions." In *The Reading Teacher*. Vol. 39, No. 3 (1985).

Clay, M. *The Early Detection of Reading Difficulties*. Portsmouth, New Hampshire: Heinemann, 1985.

Dowhower, S. "Repeated Reading: Research into Practice." In *The Reading Teacher*. Vol. 42, No. 7 (1989).

Gentile, L. & M. McMillan. *Stress and Reading Difficulties.* Newark, Delaware: International Reading Association, 1987.

Glazer, S.M. & L.B. Searfoss, Eds. *Reexamining Reading Diagnosis: New Trends and Procedures.* Newark, Delaware: International Reading Association, 1988.

Glazer, S.M. & L.B. Searfoss. *Reading Diagnosis and Instruction: A C-A-L-M Approach.* Englewood Cliffs, New Jersey: Prentice-Hall, 1988.

Harlin, R., S.E. Lipa & R. Lonberger. *The Whole Language Journey.* Markham, Ontario: Pippin, 1991.

Harste, J.C., K.G. Short & C. Burke. *Creating Classrooms for Authors.* Portsmouth, New Hampshire: Heinemann, 1988.

Johnston, P.H. & P.N. Winograd. "Passive Failure in Reading." In *Journal of Reading Behavior.* Vol. 17, No. 4 (1985).

Juel, C. "Learning to Read and Write: A Longitudinal Study of 54 Children from First through Fourth Grades." In *Journal of Educational Psychology.* Vol. 80, No. 4 (1988).

Manzo, A.V. "The Request Procedure." In *Journal of Reading.* Vol. 13, No. 2 (1969).

Mudre, L.H. & S. McCormick. "Effects of Meaning-Focused Cues on Underachieving Readers' Context Use, Self-Corrections, and Literal Comprehension." In *Reading Research Quarterly.* Vol. 24, No. 1 (1989).

Ogle, D. "K-W-L: A Teaching Model that Develops Active Reading of Expository Text." In *The Reading Teacher.* Vol. 39, No. 6 (1986).

Palinscar, A.S. & A.L. Brown. "Reciprocal Teaching of Comprehension-Fostering and Comprehension-Monitoring Activities." In *Cognition and Instruction.* Vol. 1, No. 1 (1984).

Paris, S.G. & E.R. Oka. "Strategies for Comprehending Text and Coping with Reading Difficulties." In *Learning Disability Quarterly.* Vol. 12, No. 1 (1989).

Pearson, P.D. & D.D. Johnson. *Teaching Reading Comprehension.* New York: Holt, Rinehart & Winston, 1978.

Raffini, J.P. *Student Apathy: The Protection of Self-Worth.* Washington, D.C.: National Education Association, 1988.

Santa, C.M., S.C. Dailey & M. Nelson. "Free-Response and Opinion-Proof: A Reading and Writing Strategy for Middle Grade and Secondary Teachers." In *Journal of Reading.* Vol. 28, No. 4 (1985).

Smith, F. *Joining the Literacy Club.* Portsmouth, New Hampshire: Heinemann, 1988.

Stanovich, K.E. "Matthew Effects in Reading: Some Consequences of Individual Differences in the Acquisition of Literacy." In *Reading Research Quarterly.* Vol. 21, No. 4 (1986).

Walker, B.J. *Diagnostic Teaching of Reading: Techniques for Instruction and Assessment.* 2nd Ed. Columbus, Ohio: Merrill, 1992.

Walker, B.J. *Remedial Reading.* Washington, D.C.: National Education Association, 1990.

Will, M. *Educating Students with Learning Problems: A Shared Responsibility.* Washington, D.C.: Office of Special Education and Rehabilitative Services, U.S. Department of Education, 1986.

Wixson, K.K. & M.Y. Lipson. "Reading (Dis)Abilities: An Interactionist Perspective." In *Contexts of School-Base Literacy.* (T.E. Raphael, Ed.). New York: Random House, 1986.

Wong, B.Y.L. "Understanding the Learning-Disabled Reader: Contribution from Cognitive Psychology." In *Topics in Learning and Learning Disabilities.* Vol. 4, No. 1 (1982).

THE PIPPIN TEACHER'S LIBRARY

The titles in this series are designed to provide a forum for interpreting, in clear, straightforward language, current issues and trends affecting education. Teachers are invited to share — in their own voice — the insights, wisdom and knowledge they have developed out of their professional experiences.

Submissions for publication are welcomed. Manuscripts and proposals will be reviewed by members of the Pippin Teacher's Library Editorial Advisory Board, chaired by Lee Gunderson, PhD, of the University of British Columbia.

Members of the Editorial Advisory Board are:
Karen Feathers, PhD, of Wayne State University.
Richard McCallum, PhD, of the University of California, Berkeley.
Jon Shapiro, PhD, of the University of British Columbia.
Jan Turbill, MEd, of the University of Wollongong, New South Wales.
David Wray, PhD, of the University of Exeter, England.

Written submissions should be directed to:
The Editorial Director
Pippin Publishing Corporation
85 Ellesmere Road
Suite 232
Scarborough, Ontario
Canada
M1R 4B9